Annie

101 WAYS

YOU

CAN SAVE

MONEY

Take Control of Your Financial Future!

Tanya C. Stokes

101 Ways You Can
Save Money
Take Control of Your Financial Future

**The World's Most
User-friendly
Money Saving Guide**

Tanya C. Stokes

Published by Honeycomb, Inc.

Honeycomb Publishing, Inc.
3162 Flushing Road
Flint, Michigan 48504

Cover Concept by Marilyn Farris

Cover Design by Design at Bookcovers.com

Layout Design by Karen Mackie for mackieSTUDIO@comcast.net

Manufactured in the United States of America

ISBN 978-0-9793799-0-1

DEDICATION

To the all-wise God who gives wisdom. To my husband, Timothy, who nurtured my potential, and to my lovely children: Brendon, Amber, Emmanuel, and Timothy II. To my parents, Wiley C. and the late, Georgianna Thomas, who gave me my foundation in life. To my mother-in-law, Mary Stokes, for her continual support. To my siblings: Emmo, Gail, Kimberly, Mary, and Wiley C., Jr. for standing by me. To my Family Worship Center Church-Flint family for their continual love and support. To Susan Martin, who inspired me to write this book.

SPECIAL THANKS

To a team of wonderful individuals who have made this book possible; Timothy R. Stokes, for his invaluable insight and hours spent in editing; Ed Shepard, my Senior Editor, for the hours that you labored to make this an excellent book to read; thanks, Karen Mackie for the hours that you sacrificed from beginning to end. I most certainly couldn't have completed this project in the level of excellence without your extraordinary talent; Marilyn Farris, you are a Personal Assistant like none other, thank you for helping me bring forth this product; Ted Jordan, thanks for the hours that you spent with me in the studio producing the audio version of this book, you are one of a kind. To the many others who offered their support in various ways; Maxine Murray, Lisa Banks, Rachel Hariston, Deborah Hardy, Jackie Holmes, Lenard Dotson, Mark and Angela Parker, Christina Steward for your hours of research, Deborah Nelson, Beverly Towns for continual encouragement and to everyone who purchases a copy of this book. May it enrich your life forever.

The Wisdom Inside
The World's Most User-friendly Money Saving Guide

Part I: Cashflow Management

Part II: Debt Reduction

Part III: Budgeting

Part IV: Purchasing Strategies

Part V: Investments

PREFACE

I recently read two newspaper articles that evaluated the state of Americans as it relates to our financial preparation for the future. The statistics were alarming, to say the least. Both articles painted a very bleak picture. One article indicated that only 1/3 of all workers have a savings account, or a "nest egg," for the future. It talked about how there will be no Social Security money for the Baby Boomers, and this will cause them to have to work well into their seventies just to survive.

The other article was titled, "Personal Saving Dips to Depression-Era Levels." This sums up why "101 Ways You Can Save Money" is a must. The article said that the nation's personal savings rate was a negative one percent in 2006. In other words we, as Americans, not only are not saving, on average, but we are doing more borrowing and are in debt. "There have been only two other years in history when the savings rate had fallen into this negative territory and that was 1932 and 1933, during the Great Depression. It's time to wake up America!

The two articles mentioned above, tells me that most people live from paycheck to paycheck, without any real preparation for their future in mind. The articles really speak to what the quality of life will be like or is headed toward in this country. We live in a society that has grown accustomed to abundance, but in too many cases is not accustomed to saving.

It's time to make changes now because we are behind. We often live as if money is not an issue or will not be an issue in the future. We get what we want, when we want it. Thank God that I finally learned about financial management and how to save. If I had the knowledge that I now possess twenty years ago, I would indeed be wealthy today.

Now, I know why my parents use to complain about me and my siblings wasting food. Of course, we would always hear a story about some other kids who were starving in Africa. Believe it or not, I have passed those stories on to my children in an attempt to teach them to never take things for granted. I now value what it means to pay for electricity, for example. That's why every light in the house should not be on when they're not being used.

One element of the definition of "wisdom" is *to be far-sighted.* Now is the time to look far enough ahead to anticipate what it is going to take to be prepared when we arrive in our "future." I am reminded of the parable of the wise virgins in the Bible, who had oil in their lamps and were prepared for the day that the Bridegroom returned. But, there were some foolish virgins who didn't have enough oil in their lamps and they wanted to borrow from the wise virgins who had brought extra. The wise virgins had just enough oil for the occasion. They told the foolish virgins that they had to go to the merchants and buy their own. The foolish virgins did go buy more oil, but by the time they returned they had missed the celebration. The principle here is that it is wise to be prepared and foolish not to be.

This book, "101 Ways You Can Save Money" was compiled for this reason. It encompasses tips that I have learned along the way of life in an attempt to find a successful system of financial management. Personal money management is a subject that wasn't taught in high school or college. I have gained this wisdom through life lessons. Life (wisdom) will teach you if you take the time to listen.

The goal of "101 Ways You Can Save Money" is to provide you with the skills to save on daily expenses so that you can improve your ability to save for your future. Wealthy people are wealthy because they have gained and honed the skill of managing their money. They are good at saving. The problem is not always a lack of finances, but a lack of the knowledge and skill to manage finances.

I hope that this book will be helpful, even if it simply motivates you toward finding creative ways to save. Hopefully, you will develop a strategy that works for you.

Some people think, "If I had extra money, I'd save." The purpose of this book is to teach you how to find the money, in your current income, to save. It's there! With a few adjustments and a little discipline, you should be able to find and save a significant amount of money. After sharing just one tip with a friend of mine, she made a minor adjustment in her budget and is now saving $50 per week. Before this adjustment, she claimed that she didn't have any money to save. Often, people are waiting for a large windfall of money to begin saving; but, the truth is that a little here and a little there adds up to a large sum over time.

Any one of these 101 tips can be the key to your financial breakthrough.

HOW TO USE THIS BOOK

Please begin reading this book by writing down your savings goal in the space provided. You can list a short-term, mid-range, and long-term goal. For example, a short-term goal may be to immediately free $200 per month and start saving. Your mid-range goal may be to have $30,000 saved within five years. A long-range goal may be to have $200,000 saved within ten years.

This book is designed to provide you with simple strategies to help you save. The great thing about applying these strategies is that once you get the hang of them, you'll gain the necessary momentum to save. The purpose of finding money that you can save is for it not to be consumed; therefore, I recommend that you identify at least two savings vehicles to which you can redirect your money. One account can serve as a reserve. Store about $4,000 in this account. The second account is for money that you *never* touch. This account will help you to reach your long-range goal.

Each of the 101 strategies have an "Action Point" section which allows you to create a way in which you can implement that strategy. Please take time to capture the action that you need to apply so that once you've finished reading the book, you can have your strategies outlined in order to immediately put the principles to work for you. Those strategies will then become your master savings plan.

If you're the type of person who works well with a partner, then team up with a friend and challenge each other to attain financial success. You can lean on each other's strengths and receive encouragement in the time of need.

My goal is for you to build savings habits into your life to ensure lasting victory. Have fun reading "101 Ways You Can Save Money" and enjoy your journey to success one day at a time!

Your Saving Goal

	Goal	Amount to Save	Projected Achievement Date
Short-Term	_____	$_____	_____
Mid-Range	_____	$_____	_____
Long-Term	_____	$_____	_____

Part I

Cashflow Management

1

---

managing money

*J*n this section we deal with cashflow management. Here, we offer several tips on ways to protect your money from being consumed. Ignorance is costly, especially when it comes to managing money. At different points in my life I have learned each one of the 101 savings tips listed in this book, mostly as the result of trial and error. This one, "Managing Money," is no exception. Ignorance of these principles has cost me tens of thousands of dollars through the years.

wisdom for wealth

Managing money is the key to wealth.

Earning money was never a problem for me and neither was spending money. Saving money was challenging because I usually didn't have much money left to save. Every time someone wastes money, it is the result of either ignorance (not knowing better) or foolishness (lacking wisdom). Money lost is money that could have been saved. There are five key areas of knowledge and skill relative to money management: cashflow management, debt reduction, budgeting, purchasing strategies, and investments.

I believe that there is skill involved in managing money and this skill can be learned. This skill definitely did not come easily for me and in looking at the lives of so many others, it does not appear to be common knowledge. It is a skill; however, that one must acquire to be successful with finances.

One of the reasons that most people don't have significant savings is that it takes effort and discipline to manage money for savings. To be disciplined is to follow a course. Financial success is setting the right financial course and following it. This tip, and many more of these, is valuable not only in the money that it allows you to save, but also in that it helps you develop the discipline that brings financial success.

The difference between wealthy people and others is that wealthy people "manage" their money. It is impossible to have financial success without going through the effort and discipline of managing money.

Your*A*ction *P*oint

2

---

a saver's mentality

*B*eing an effective saver is an acquired skill. It takes what I call a "saver's mentality" to apply this skill. The problem is that if you have not been conditioned to save, either by instruction or by constant exposure to people who practiced the art of saving, then doing this will probably not come naturally for you. In fact, for example, two-thirds of Americans aren't saving toward retirement. This means that most people can live a lifetime without building a "saver's mentality" into their lifestyle.

With the instability of our economy and other factors causing the high cost of living, it has become increasingly more difficult to save. Home mortgages are skyrocketing. Energy bills are so high that you want to turn off your heat in the middle of a Michigan winter. The cost of groceries rivals that of other major expenses. This forces you, if you are wise, to find creative strategies of saving to avoid living from paycheck to paycheck. How many weeks can you live without receiving a paycheck? This is an indication of your current financial strength. What is the "saver's mentality?" It is the opposite mindset of a "spender." A spender releases money with little regard for his or her future status. Spenders don't anticipate unexpected expenses or plan for future financial security. A saver stores money with a clear view of the future in mind. A saver often delays purchases to avoid taxing his or her disposable income. Disposable income is the money that you have available to you for spending. Savers are disciplined money managers. It is important to them that they have money, even more than things. Most people don't want to experience financial lack or have to work all of their lives; however, their daily money habits create this exact outcome.

I'm a "bottom-line" person, you have to begin by; 1) being honest with yourself about the results that you are getting, not the ones that you desire; look at your savings account to judge whether you are a saver or a spender; 2) you then must be willing to change your mentality based on the results you desire. Do something about your situation other than just "feel bad." I have labored mentally over my financial life. I have also read many books on finances in order to be equipped to win the financial game. It wasn't until I took on a certain mentality--the "saver's mentality"-- that things began to change for me. The information that I read was very helpful, but it was a decision that brought significant change. I have a simple focus for this book; to motivate you to take on a "saver's mentality." If you are already saving, then you'll find tips and strategies to increase your savings.

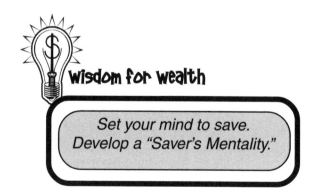

wisdom for wealth

Set your mind to save.
Develop a "Saver's Mentality."

Your Action Point

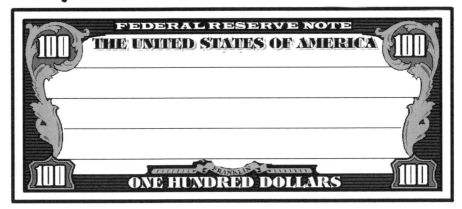

101 ways you can save money

3

---

cut and save

*J*n each savings tip there is a two step approach. The first is to cut--minimizing your expenses. The second is to save--actually taking the difference from what you would have spent and putting it into some type of savings vehicle. To cut expenses without exercising the discipline of actually putting the money into some type of savings vehicle will cause you to suffer on one end without realizing the benefit on the other.

If you can calculate the savings realized, especially if it's on a reoccuring expense, then factor that into the amount that you plan to save. For instance, if you save $40 a week by taking a lunch instead of dining out every day, then you should plan to put at least $160 per month into some type of savings vehicle. Believe it or not, in a year you'll have saved $2,080 ($40 x 52 weeks).

In order to accelerate your savings, eliminate all unnecessary spending. Remember, you want to take time to build the "saver's mentality" into your daily routine. The previous example demonstrates the power of cutting expenses not by starving, but by just using a different strategy to accomplish the same goal and saving all the while.

Identify savings vehicles, such as interest-bearing bank accounts into which you can deposit savings once you cut your expenses. Many of the tips that I have selected for this book involve cutting expenses, and I want you to know that cutting can always yield savings.

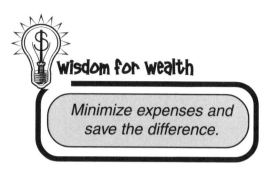

wisdom for wealth

Minimize expenses and save the difference.

Your Action Point

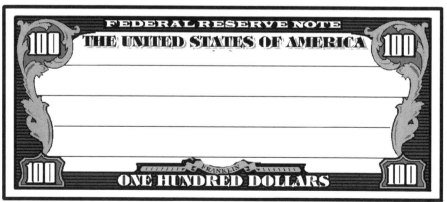

4

play the money game

Some people figuratively refer to money as a "game." There are even literal games on the market that attempt to teach money management concepts. I would recommend that you buy those games and learn more about your money mentality. I've learned a lot about myself playing such games. If you look at money from the perspective of it being a game, then why not learn to play and play to win? Our objective is to get ahead and stay ahead of the game.

In this season of my life, I'm literally challenging myself to save as much as I possibly can. Since I've made it a focus, I am much more successful at saving (and holding on to it) than in times past. If I come up short, I strategize on how I can get around touching my savings accounts. As a result of this challenge, I make different choices. I now wait on things that I would have normally just purchased. Such restraint is building in me the discipline that I need for long-term financial success.

You can play the money game by first committing to learn everything that you can about the game. Knowledge empowers. Play the game until you figure out how it works and find a strategy that works for you.

There are three phases to the money game; earn (gather), manage (spend), and save/invest (store). A weakness in any one of these phases can cause you to lose the money game. You need an aggressive and balanced attack.

Instead of allowing money to control your emotions, play the game. Don't let money dictate to your self esteem or your future. Relax and have fun while you play. Don't be afraid to get in the game. When you play, play to win. Be a fierce and strategic competitor. Go ahead: work up a sweat and save hard. Learn to make your money work for you harder than you work to earn it.

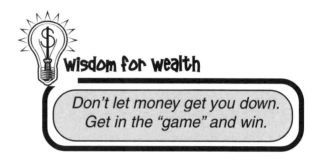

wisdom for wealth

*Don't let money get you down.
Get in the "game" and win.*

Your*A*ction *P*oint

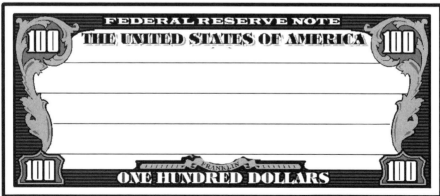

5

get help!

*T*he right kind of help at the right time is priceless! When I don't know something I search for answers. I always find them in people who have walked that path before. It's wise to seek help.

You may have to go outside of your normal circle of friends. They may not have all of the answers that you need. The right advice can save you tons of money simply by avoiding costly mistakes while at the same time making the right choices. This can put you years ahead in financial management.

wisdom for wealth

What you don't know can hurt you. Get Help!

Think about it this way, if you are traveling down the highway headed in the wrong direction, which I've done before in unfamiliar places, you are much further behind than when you entered onto that course. For instance, if you travel 30 minutes in the wrong direction, it will take you 30 minutes just to get back to where you started. In this example, you didn't lose 30 minutes, but an hour (again, just to get back where you started).

If you had traveled in the right direction, you would be an hour closer to your destination. So, it's really two hours that was lost because it's going to take you traveling another hour in order to get to where you would have been had you been traveling in the right direction from the start. What a major difference it makes when you're on the right course! The same is true with finances. Traveling on the right financial course can result in you being years ahead of where you would have been had you not been on the right course.

I was 28 when my first child was born. I called my mother and desperately asked, "How did you do this?" She raised six children. I didn't have a clue about how to properly raise my son, so I sought the knowledge that I needed. I use the same approach in seeking financial wisdom from successful people.

If your bank book is screaming, "Get a Clue!" then seek the help that you need. It's better to admit that you need help than to keep doing the same thing, but expecting different results. That's the definition of insanity. Your aim is RESULTS!

Your Action Point

6

insurance gives assurance

*T*he proper insurance can be a life saver and a money saver. I am particularly referring to insurance purchased to protect assets, such as homeowner's insurance. I know two people who experienced the same calamity in the same city. Both had insurance, but one was covered and the other was not. One policy saved the owner, but the other policy cost the owner dearly. It is best to be familiar with your policy and all the details of its coverage. Check out your insurance policies. Go through them with a fine-tooth comb. Pay attention to the small print.

I recently came home from a vacation to a flooded basement due to a Sump Pump failure caused by a power outage. "Not another problem," was my first reaction, not knowing whether it would be covered under my insurance policy or not. I had valuable exercise equipment down there, along with several boxes of new furniture that I was saving for our upcoming move. I was

wisdom for wealth

Cover your blind spots. Know your insurance coverage well!

quite relieved to find that it was covered under our insurance policy. Ironically, our friends returned home from their vacation with the exact problem. Their damage wasn't covered under their insurance policy.

The damage in our situation was such that our entire 2600 square foot basement had to be gutted. We had just gotten new drywall and flooring installed because we were preparing to list the house. Listen closely here: I had the same insurance that my friends had, but I switched insurances upon the recommendation of a builder. I needed liability insurance on some land that I had purchased and the previous policy did not offer it, so I switched. I switched because it met my needs in one area, but I really didn't review my policy to see all of what it covered for my current home. Had I not switched then, my property would not have been covered. The loss would have been in excess of $65,000. Knowing the terms of your insurance coverage will save you in the long run.

I have since learned that our policy had unlimited coverage when it comes to loss and damage of that nature. Although the premiums of the policies were comparable, there was no comparison in the coverage. Make sure that your policy covers common mishaps in your region of the country, such as damage done by snow, heavy rains, and other weather related causes.

Your Action Point

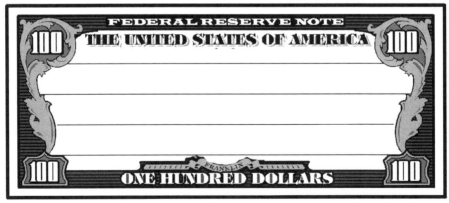

7

sweat the small stuff

One key to protecting your cashflow is paying attention to detail. Heightened attention ensures savings in a variety of ways. Reviewing your receipts after purchases can save money. By the way, it is customary for stores that use scanners to offer rewards for mistakes that are caught. Notice that I said mistakes "that are caught." Know if there was a mistake made and realize significant savings. Generally there is a ten dollar maximum that you can receive for such scanning mistakes. I have caught such mistakes, gone to the service counter to report it and have gotten paid. You not only get the money back that you lost due to the error, but you also get the "bonus" money.

wisdom for wealth

It pays to be financially alert, especially when you are shopping.

Shopping just before a holiday presents its own challenges. The grocery lines are long and all you want to do is get in and out quickly. This is probably why I missed what happened to me during one of these holiday excursions. I paid for my groceries and left the store. A couple of days later, I pulled out a pack of chicken legs (six to be exact) that I bought at the meat counter. I would normally open the package and discard it immediately, but this particular day the price sticker caught my eye. It read, "You pay $35.44." I couldn't believe my eyes, so I read it again. I told my husband in disbelief. He was stunned. I realized that it was the butcher's error, but thank God that I caught the error and still had my receipt to prove it. I quickly returned to the store to receive my full reimbursement for the $35.44 chicken legs—WOW! What a lesson I learned about paying attention to details when handling money. That was money that would have been lost had I not caught the error.

Make a habit of counting the change that you receive back from a purchase. Sometimes it may seem uncomfortable to count in front of the cashier, but he or she counts your money in front of you. Cashiers make mistakes too. This is why I train my children to count their change to make sure that it's correct.

Thoroughly check all of your receipts, credit card statements, bank statements, and investment statements. Trust me, mistakes happen all of the time; don't let them happen at your expense.

Your *A*ction *P*oint

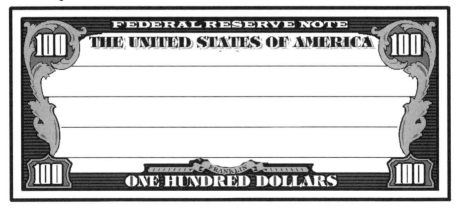

8

save your change

*O*ne way to get in the "habit" of saving is to save your change. If you think about it, you probably spend money every day. So, if you spend every day then why not save every day as well? When you spend daily and acquire loose change, save that change daily until you build this habit into your life. I have done this for years. You will be amazed at how quarters, dimes, nickels and pennies add up over time. I've read of people who have saved change and were able to use it to pay cash for brand new vehicles. My family has a general principle that we don't spend change. It is even an effective way to condition children to save.

Once, I saved my change for a year and gave it to someone as a gift for her newborn baby. It was more than $500! Save your change to establish a habit of saving, but you

wisdom for wealth

If you spend every day, you can save every day by saving change.

also want to have a goal in mind for its use. We generally use our change for special things like Christmas shopping. Last year, we divided the change among our four children and opened their first money management accounts. If you wish, you can save the change and put it in a long-term savings account at the end of each year.

Again, this is a simple, yet very effective strategy for building the savings habit into your life.

Your**A**ction **P**oint

9

pay yourself first

*T*his is probably one of the best savings strategies. The issue is that if you haven't been able to save then ALL of your money is being consumed. Paying yourself first gives you the feeling of freedom. If your money is going to be gone by the end of the month anyhow, then at least you are saving along the way. One way to accomplish this is through a financial advisor. I have investments that automatically come out of my account each month. This is a good system because you do not have immediate access to the money; therefore, you are more likely not to touch it.

Automatic withdrawals into company 401k's or other investment vehicles right off the top are literally good ways to pay yourself first. When I first heard about this concept, it made sense to me because if you pay yourself last then there may not be anything left. By paying yourself first you make your financial welfare a priority.

Some advisors don't recommend saving when you have debt. Their logic is that it's best to eliminate the debt first, because of what you're losing in interest. From my experience, it's best to have savings set aside while eliminating debt. As advised, I stopped saving ten percent of my income in an effort to accelerate becoming debt free. Based on this decision, I found myself back in debt and without a savings because I had not changed my mentality. If I had maintained my original course of savings, over a ten year period, I would have accumulated more than $96,000 in principle (without adding compound interest) and at the same time eliminating debt.

If you can begin by paying yourself 10 percent of your monthly income, then you're on your way to long-term financial strength. If not 10 percent, then find a percentage that works for you and commit to saving. It really adds up over time. You need the patience to let it grow. You can use any extra or unexpected money to tackle your debt faster.

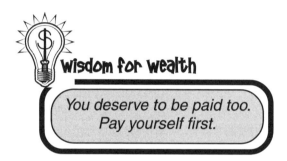

wisdom for wealth

You deserve to be paid too. Pay yourself first.

I heard of one woman who started her savings plan with only a dollar a month. Then it doubled and multiplied until she had saved hundreds of thousands of dollars. The point is that she started with what she had and with the help of pure determination to save, she then found ways to increase from there.

Your **A**ction **P**oint

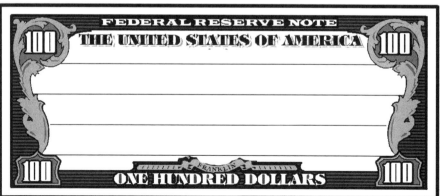

10

the power of a list

Unplanned spending is one of the greatest enemies to saving and grocery shopping is a perfect set up for unplanned spending. These days, you can spend your entire paycheck in a grocery store, especially at these "super" stores. Making a list for your grocery shopping adds focus to the mission and gives you the platform to fight impulses. It keeps you on your course because grocery stores are set up to encourage you to spend. This is done from the way items are displayed, to "impulse items" at checkout, to the music playing over the in-

wisdom for wealth

Let your list be your guide.

tercom system. Based on research that they've done, they play music that encourages you to spend. They have a plan to get your money, but your list protects your plan to keep it.

When I have shopped without my list I have often wondered, after spending more than expected, what I really got in terms of real meals. The extras that find their way into your grocery cart can drastically inflate your bill. The primary purpose of grocery shopping is to purchase the things that you need along with a few items that you want; however, when you don't have a list you get all the things that you want and usually forget the few things that you really need.

You may want to keep an ongoing list on the refrigerator as a starter because it is very difficult to remember everything that you need once you're in the store. If you use the list for the purpose of tracking essentials then this can automatically scale down the unnecessary items and produce savings.

YourAction Point

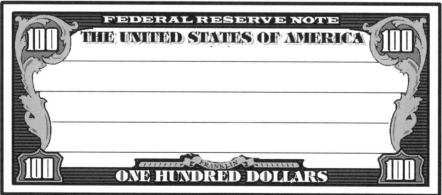

11

shop the market

*J*grew up visiting the local Farmer's Market with my mother. She bought our fresh fruits and vegetables from the Market every Saturday. This taught me how to buy quality food, but I didn't necessarily think of it from a financial point of view.

Today, many years later, a visit to the local Market can still prove worthwhile. When I moved back to my hometown after years of being away, I automatically found a good grocery store nearby and eventually I found my way back to the Farmer's Market. I could literally take about $50 with me and "clean up." On the other hand, any time I shopped at the grocery store I would easily spend $150.

wisdom for wealth

Shopping at the Market still makes good financial sense.

The Market helps to keep you on course with your spending because you can normally avoid the "extras;" 1) you don't have the hands to carry much and 2) the Market does not have nearly the selection or the variety, not to mention the "attractions," that you find in the large su-permarkets.

More and more people are becoming aware of the cost-cutters the Market affords because there is constant traffic when I go now. They had to expand the parking lot due to the traffic. I love to get fresh fruit, vegetables, and meat from the Market. What excites me the most is what I save.

Your**A**ction **P**oint

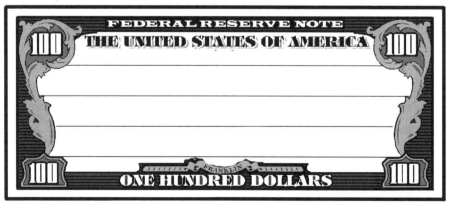

12

---

the recipe for saving

Here's the "recipe" for saving money--cook. Some people have the natural gift to cook. They absolutely love it, and so does everyone who sits at their dining table. Then there are others, like me, who cook because if they didn't, they would starve. For these people, life is challenging. Two things are working against them: lack of knowledge and lack of creativity, both of which can be costly.

When my creativity reaches its limit in the kitchen, then pizza looks really good. Eating out for a family of six; however, is costly. I've concluded that cooking skills save you money. So, revive the cook in you.

wisdom for wealth

Revive the
COOK
in you.

If I order Chinese food, a dinner costs us about twenty-two dollars. I could have had about two meals or more for that price by cooking at home. There are times when I just don't want to cook, but when considering my options I have to revive the cook in me. I used to vacillate between the cost of home cooking and eating out. From a financial point of view, I'm convinced that homecooking wins over eating out.

Your*A*ction *P*oint

13

---

avoid neglect

*T*he main reason that I wrote this book is to pass along tips that I've gathered over the years about finances and money management. Many of these lessons I have learned through the "School of Hard Knocks." I graduated Summa Cum Laude and I've got the splinters to prove it. I don't mind sharing so that you can avoid graduation day. I believe in education, but in this instance, I'm encouraging you to drop out.

It wasn't until after living in our home for nine years that we considered updating. We had signs all around us as indicators that upgrading was long overdue. It's not that the house was falling apart, it just didn't have the kind of attention that it required from homeowners. It needed new paint, new tile flooring, an upgraded bathroom, etc. We addressed several remodeling issues (some of which were urgent) in a relatively short time. It takes years to recover from this--trust me! Had I done a little upgrading at a time, it wouldn't have taken such a chunk out of my savings account all at once.

Neglect is allowing something to remain the same. Neglect is costly. The small drip in the bathtub will become a waterfall, complete with rainbow, if you let it. Your plumber will be the only one who's happy.

Create a regular maintenance schedule for items like cars, heating and cooling units and major appliances. Make sure that your electrical systems, plumbing and roof are up-to-date and in good working condition. Consistently upgrade areas that most directly affect property value, such as kitchens, bathrooms, exterior paint, and interior decorating issues like wall paper, paint, and window treatments. If you have a basement, make sure you don't have any leaks.

wisdom for wealth

Neglect is costly.
Maintain your home,
appliances and vehicles.

Keep your down spouts in good condition because if the water doesn't drain away from the house, it will find its way into the house.

Anything that is subject to regular use will wear out over time. You want to monitor items and be able to schedule their replacement, or repair rather than experience unexpected breakdowns, which will become untimely expenses. It's all about management. The longer you wait to address regular maintenance items, the more costly the repair. Have you ever noticed something that was not that big of a deal turn into a major repair because of neglect?

Your **A**ction **P**oint

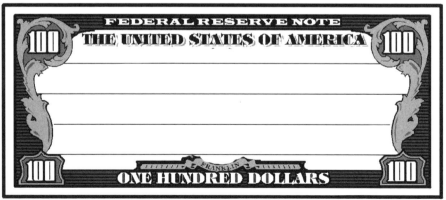

14

---

retire your money clip

*T*his tip comes from my personal experience with my husband. Somewhere he picked up the idea that carrying a money clip was cool. Yes, I think carrying a money clip is cool too, but my issue came when he wanted it full at all times. The problem is the mentality that followed the clip. Having a lot of cash gives you multiple opportunities to spend. It invites spending. Instead of carrying around hundreds of dollars waiting on an opportunity to be spent, we could have put that excess cash in an account gaining interest.

My husband never carries much money, but in an attempt to fill the clip, he began carrying hundreds of dollars. When he spent money or gave it away (which was most of the time), then he would replenish the clip. We couldn't control that system and he couldn't give an account of the money. He remembered some things, like the person whom he helped get his car fixed, but couldn't really remember the rest. My husband is a giver, so having that kind of money available every week wasn't good.

Our financial life was rescued. Today, his clip is retired and living the high life in the bottom of a nice, cushy drawer. When we reach our financial goals, then I might let it out of retirement.

wisdom for wealth

Reduce available cash for unplanned spending: carry around with you only the money that you truly need each day.

Your *Action Point*

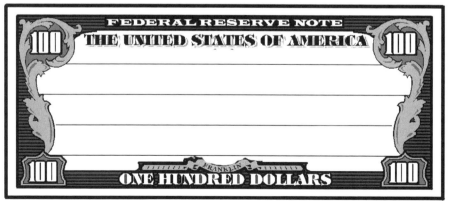

15

---

convenience costs!

*I*t might be beneficial for you to lay aside the "convenience mentality" once and for all and save. The dictionary defines *convenience* as "that which gives ease; accommodation; that which is suitable to want or necessity; freedom from difficulty."

This convenience seems to lurk around nearly every corner in life. Your wants or necessities can be purchased with little or no difficulty. Neighborhood convenience stores serve that very purpose, quick and easy. The only thing that you need to be sensitive to is that convenience costs! This convenience may seem easy up front, but it can be painful to your budget on the back end.

I have gone in convenience stores for an essential item and after looking at the price, set the item back down. It's hard for me to pay double for less trouble. Something within, probably my saver's mentality, does not allow me to spend like that. I think it's just the principle of paying twice the price for the same item. I don't think so. High price convenience items are ear-marked for people who lack order in their lives. They try to make it seem as if it is a blessing. Just bop in and pay rather than travel down the street to the grocery store. I have returned to my vehicle and driven a mile down the road to the local grocery store for the item.

If the thought comes to mind, "this is so convenient," then beware of what it's costing you. A friend informed me that she purchased hot apple cider daily from a drive-thru convenience-type business. It cost her $1.69 five times a week, totaling $8.45 per week, $33.80 per month, and $405.60 per year. Because she was blinded by the convenience, she never even considered the cost until now.

Many people don't even have $400 in savings; yet, she was blowing her

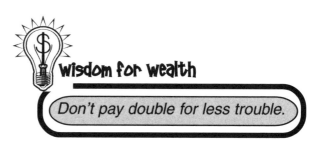

wisdom for wealth

Don't pay double for less trouble.

savings potential on cider. This is an example of how there is money that can be saved when you eliminate buying convenience items. After reading a manuscript of this book, she decided to just buy a box of apple cider, in individual packets and warm it up herself. She was able to purchase a two week supply for only $1.50. She spent $3 a month instead of $33.80. You do the math! The key is that she was buying the apple cider daily without even considering what that convenience was costing her. Notice, she was still able to drink apple cider daily, while experiencing tremendous savings. Can you name one convenience that is costing you? Utilize a different purchasing strategy and save the excess.

Your Action Point

16

atm's

I renamed the "Automatic Teller Machine" the "Automatic Taking Machine." When I first began using ATM's I thought that they were good because of the convenience. I didn't realize what this "easy access" system was costing me. I now rarely use ATM's.

You can save on fees that you're charged when using ATM's that aren't associated with your local bank. ATM's can absolutely destroy your cashflow when you frequently use them. They can exploit your money management weaknesses.

wisdom for wealth

Easy come, easy go; avoid using ATM's.

ATM cards can be very difficult to manage if record-keeping isn't your strength. It's easy to forget withdrawals that you've made and what's worse is when your spouse makes withdrawals without your knowledge. You talk about a recipe for disaster! This can throw your account into a deficit which costs even more in Insufficient Funds Fees. The cost of a mistake is phenomenal these days.

More importantly, you are more prone to be a spendthrift if you use your ATM card often. Resist the temptation of spending unnecessarily. Leave home without it or just carry it in case of "real emergencies."

Make sure that your use of ATM's is in line with your budget. If you run to the ATM with no forethought of its impact on your budget, then it is time to retire your card to minimize your losses.

I have friends who have serious financial problems who use ATM's almost daily. Regular ATM use is a habit of poor money managers in that it is usually tied to unplanned spending. If you manage money properly, then you won't have to run to the ATM's. Regular ATM use is usually part of an undisciplined financial lifestyle.

Your*A*ction *P*oint

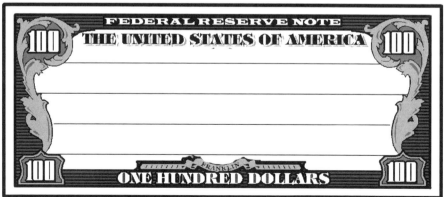

17

delay for payday

*I*n my opinion, the paycheck advance business, more than any other business, preys on the feelings of desperation of people with financial problems.

If you ever want to make a bad situation worse, then take an advance on your paycheck. One sign that paycheck advance businesses are a part of a poor financial strategy is that they are popping up in large numbers in low income areas, but they are rarely seen in affluent areas.

Let me ask you a question. If you feel as though you cannot wait until payday to receive your paycheck, can you afford to receive your paycheck less 12– 15 percent? Obviously, if you are considering going to a paycheck advance business, then you don't have enough money. By going to a paycheck advance business, you will have less than not enough money—faster.

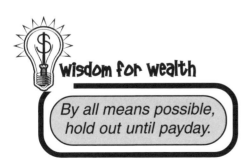

wisdom for wealth

By all means possible, hold out until payday.

Your Action Point

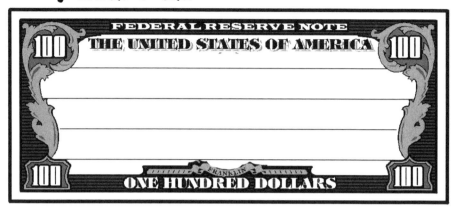

18

---

plan vacations ahead

*B*efore you know it vacation time is here. Are you finan-cially prepared? If not, last minute arrangements can be very costly. I've ended up in the vacation crunch more than once, when my body was telling me that it's time for a break, but my money was saying, "Not now." The remedy is—plan ahead.

I've admired people who can tell you their life's schedule a year in advance. Though I am a planner, I have never seemed to plan that far ahead. I have proven more than once that planning ahead is critical to vacation savings.

I recently read a newspaper article of one woman's story about her vacation. She had $1000 to work with for a family of four. In the end, because she researched activities, purchased tickets ahead and found the best hotel deals, she experienced a quality vacation with her budget still intact. I was absolutely impressed.

Airline tickets are normally cheaper when purchased at least thirty days in advance. This is added incentive to plan ahead. One trip cost us over two thousand dollars more because we didn't plan far enough in advance. We were going to use a timeshare ex-change, but we were informed that we needed to have called at least six months beforehand. Not only did we pay more, but our accommodations were far inferior to what they would have been. Point taken! Plan far enough in advance to save as much as you can and have a good time.

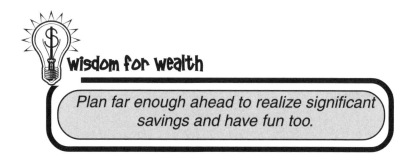

wisdom for wealth

Plan far enough ahead to realize significant savings and have fun too.

Your*A*ction *P*oint

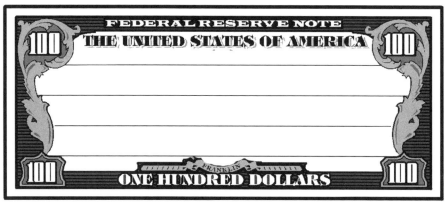

19

simplify and save

Simplicity of life saves. *Simplicity* means "singleness; the state of being unmixed or uncompounded." It also means "the state of being not complex." Almost every woman that I know is looking for the answer to this one, "How do I simplify my lifestyle?"

Here's a tip: the more stuff that you have the more it costs you and the more time it takes to manage your life. More is not always better. Simplifying your life increases your savings primarily in two ways: 1) in purchase prices and fees for activities and 2) in travel and maintenance. Everything that you buy requires some type of maintenance. The greatest benefit of simplicity may be peace of mind.

Release activities that cost more than they are worth. One summer I ran the kids around from activity to activity. They were involved in everything! I ran myself ragged. It cost a lot of money, and I'm not really sure if all of that activity was necessary. Last summer I selected one or two things for each child and was done with it. Kids are kids, and they love fun. Think of some creative, stay-at-home activities. I won a little ball for my five-year-old son, and he enjoyed just spending time playing catch. It was simple. My point is that this activity was simple, free, and it accomplished the goal without the complexities of feeling as if kids have to be in an organized, costly activity all day.

My oldest sister told me that when her three children were young, she couldn't keep up with all the laundry because they had too many clothes. She implemented a strategy to only purchase seven outfits for each of them. This was simple. Instead of everyone having too much, they had just enough and it was manageable. She saved lots of money on clothing, laundry detergent, water, energy, and kept her budget intact.

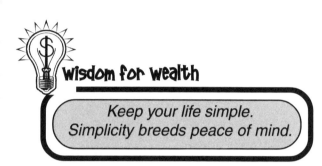

wisdom for wealth

Keep your life simple.
Simplicity breeds peace of mind.

Your Action Point

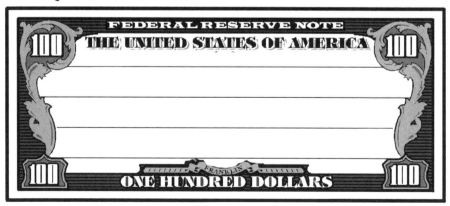

20

---

refunds and rebates

*D*on't ignore refunds and rebates regardless of the amount. Take back your refundable cans instead of trashing them. Send in the mail-in rebates, though it may only be three dollars.

The principle is that they are giving you funds back. Receive them back and bank them. Even if you give the money to the kids for a snack or something, it's money that you don't have to spend, so therefore you save. Respect the small sums just as you would the large sums.

My husband recently purchased a phone and received $125 in rebates. Do you think that we took time to send those rebates in? Most certainly!

wisdom for wealth

Receive all money that's given back to you.

We send in all rebates. For many items, such as phones and computers, the displayed price often includes mail-in rebates. Manufacturers are probably banking on the fact that many people won't take the time to send them in.

Remember this: wealthy people don't turn money away. One wealthy speaker at a conference told us of how he spotted a quarter on the floor in the airport and was hoping no one else saw it before he picked it up. He had respect for money.

Your*A*ction *P*oint

21

---

accountability

*T*he first thing that you need to do is create an effective financial plan and identify someone to whom you will be accountable that will help you carry it out. Check in periodically with the person to give a report on your progress. You may have to eat some humble pie in order to expose your true financial condition, but it will be to your benefit. My husband and I are accountable to each other financially. We have always worked together in making financial decisions, especially the major ones.

Since I have to give an account of the budget, I handle things differently. I try harder to stick to the plan. I'm more diligent about finding avenues to save. If it were not for accountability I would do what I wanted, when I wanted. Accountability safeguards you against

wisdom for wealth

Give an account now, for it may save you later. Be accountable to someone.

yourself and saves you from minor and major money mistakes. I am not saying that you have to get permission to handle your hard-earned dollar. I'm just saying accountability helps to keep you on course. Having many counselors, aids in protecting you from failure.

Having a financial partner is like having a workout partner. If you know that you have someone counting on you to show up and workout, then you're more likely to show up. Accountability places you in a position to receive that boost that you need. Try it for a while and see if it helps your portfolio.

Your *Action Point*

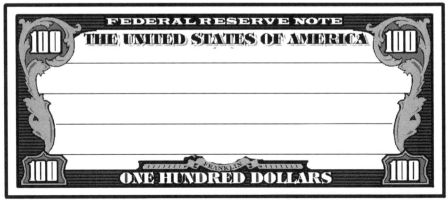

22

cut costly habits

*H*abits are built into human nature. The only problem is that some are good and some are bad. Financial success probably has more to do with your habits than anything else. What are your spending habits? What are your savings habits? What are your management habits? Once something becomes a habit, it's done automatically. What I would like for you to do is consider your habits; this will lead you to understanding the results that you are getting financially.

You're not going to eliminate the fact that you have habits, but you can change the habits that you have. Once you discover your money habits, you can make the necessary adjustments. There are some money habits that are costly: overspending and compulsion (buying what you want when you want it, regardless of the price that you have to pay). You can redirect your habits to be fueled by a mentality of saving and turn your financial picture around. Habits are just that powerful.

wisdom for wealth

Exercise the habit of saving.

If upon evaluating your money habits you discover that you have costly habits, then my advice is to cut your costly habits. Costly habits may include: smoking, drinking coffee or pop, snacks, dining out, alcohol or drug use, gambling and the like. I read a newspaper article about a woman who stopped smoking and saved the money that she was spending on cigarettes and bought a home. This is an example of how to redirect your habits to strengthen your financial picture.

If you have a habit that is costing $5 per day, you are spending $1,825 every year to support that habit. What if your habits are costing $10 per day? That equals $3,650 a year. This is money that you might not have considered that could actually be saved.

Your *A*ction *P*oint

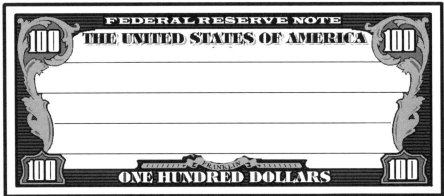

23

---

less is better

You save when you spend less. This is a simple, but profound truth that is often overlooked. By "less" I mean "of lower value in quantity and/or quality." For instance, you can get a very nice quality vehicle for less than the top-of-the-line item. I am amazed that you can pay as much, if not more, for a car as you would for a house. A car simply serves as transportation to get you from point A to point B. No matter how the car is marketed and what its amenities are, it is still a car.

I am not advocating that you cannot at some point enjoy the fruit of your labor. I'm just saying that first things should be first. If you are sacrificing your savings by overspending, then take time to establish financial order so that you don't have to work all of your life to pay for the purchase.

I believe in buying quality items to avoid repurchasing because the item falls apart easily. There should be some limits as to how far one will go. This principle works for everything you buy. You can also

wisdom for wealth

Spend less
and save more.

save when it comes to the quantity of items purchased. I know people who find something that they like and they buy one in every color. They may be able to afford purchasing in those quantities, but for most of us, this would not be the best use of our money. Even if it is affordable, limit your quantity and save.

Don't end up peering into your closet and seeing suits, shirts, ties, coats, shoes and purses with the tags still on them because you never found accessories or garments to match them. This is an indicator that you obviously could have done without the purchase and saved!

Your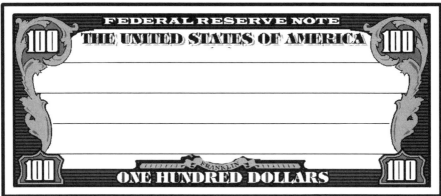ction Point

24

---

online banking

*O*nline banking has taken my money management skills to the next level. It has given me the convenience of actually watching my accounts daily. This differs drastically from reconciling upon receiving a monthly statement.

I catch errors easily and can resolve them before they cost me in fees. For instance, I authorized a company to make automatic withdrawals from my account--(arranging automatic withdrawls for investments is one of my savings strategies). One day I noticed that a large draft had cleared my account a week ahead of time. I'm glad that the money was there to cover it, but in my investigation I found that the company was set to withdraw it the next week as well. By just observing my accounts online I was able to divert the near catastrophe of up to $29 per bounced check. To make a long story short, this is just one example of what I have caught that would have slipped by had I not had online banking. You can also add the automatic bill payment feature for free or a

wisdom for wealth

Watch your money daily and save.

minimal payment that could save on postage. You have to do the math on that one. Online banking also affords you savings by eliminating trips to the bank(s) by performing most of your banking transactions online. With direct deposit and online banking I can manage my money from home or even from out of state and drastically reduce my trips to the bank.

Your*A*ction *P*oint

25

---

count before
you commit

*O*ver-commitment is a major financial problem. It's a main reason for the high credit card debt that our nation is experiencing. People are over-committing and finding it difficult, if not impossible to pay back their commitment. Over-commitment causes cashflow constraints which make you vulnerable to any unforeseen expenses.

There are times that we've verbally committed ourselves without proper forethought and have had to pay dearly. My husband is good for doing this with our kids. Even if you forget, kids certainly don't. The day after school ended last year my kids

wisdom for wealth

Close your mouth and save.

rushed to count their school supplies. I went to see what all the chatter was about and discovered that their dad had issued a challenge. My husband had reason to believe that they weren't going to keep up with their supplies for an entire year. He told them that he would give them a dollar for every school supply that they kept until the end of the year.

My thirteen-year-old said, "Dad owes me $100," and my nine-year-old followed, "Dad owes me $50." Well, the only problem is that I handle the finances, and I did not know that their dad made that commitment. Needless to say, we had to pay.

Speaking before you count can be costly. It's important to watch over your words because this can save you. I knew that since my husband had made that verbal commitment, we most certainly had to follow through. That's not the first time that he's done that with the kids. My advice to him is to watch his mouth.

Every time that you make a commitment your reputation is also on the line and in some cases so is your credit rating. Before you commit consider these things: the amount of the commitment, the timing, the length of the obligation, finance charges, and your other obligations. This could potentially save you thousands of dollars.

Your Action Point

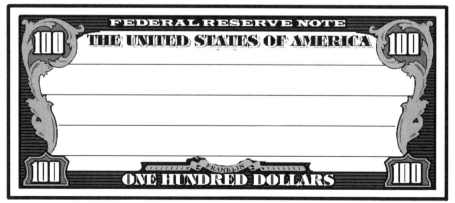

26

---

back out of being a back-up!

A good planner always has a Plan A and B. Have you ever had a relationship where you felt like you were someone's plan B? If you felt like that, it probably was true. I love to help people when I'm called upon, but there have been many times that I've helped someone else and I really didn't have it to give. At the time, I didn't see it that way, but at the end of the month when I came up short I got a revelation.

I have seen people totally wreck their financial status trying to rescue someone in a financial crisis. They became financial martyrs to save someone who usually found himself in another financial crisis the next month. Being a "back-up" can have major financial consequences. This is one sure way to exhaust your savings.

If someone comes to you regularly for financial refuge and you really don't have it to give, then back out of being the "back-up." Talk with the person about options other than you. You are not responsible for this person financially, so don't feel guilty about not being able to be used as a resource.

I had a relative who needed a car. A couple of my siblings wanted to buy him a vehicle and they wanted me to pitch in as well. I saw that if I helped with buying the car then I'd also have to help with additional related costs. Because of the person's financial condi-

tion I had to consider the long-term financial commitment. I would have had to help with gas, mainte-nance, insurance and reg-istration costs. I decided that it was more than I was willing or able to commit.

wisdom for wealth

Avoid harmful financial entanglements.

My siblings pitched in to buy the vehicle and were offended by my nonparticipation. As foreseen, the next month the vehicle was parked and rendered inoperative.

Know when you can help and when you can't. You're not the bad guy.

Your*A*ction *P*oint

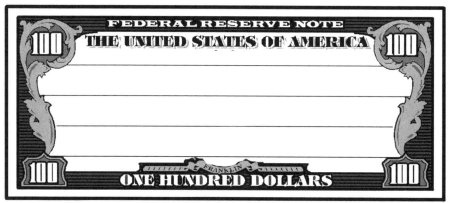

27

don't overcook

*I*n my house, leftovers often remain leftovers until I woefully put them out of their misery with a quick funeral in the garbage disposal. As a result, I've learned ways to save by reducing the amount that I cook. You can do this over time by paying attention to details. I now stop to think about how much each person eats of certain items based on history and habit. This eliminates the waste of throwing away significant amounts of food weekly.

My family loves variety, which amounts to different types of foods at each daily meal. Instead of cooking every day, you can increase your meal quantity and creatively use the leftovers other days of the week. Today's main course can be tomorrow's side dish. My goal is to not waste food as a result of overcooking. This method has saved me from wasteful purchases at the grocery store.

wisdom for wealth

Overcooking can blow your budget.

There is something about the body's craving for food that can cause us to sometimes overindulge. Remember that food expense has become a major budget item; consequently, overcooking can take you over budget.

Your*A*ction *P*oint

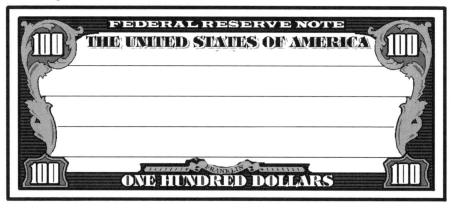

28

the reward
of re-wear

If you grew up wearing "hand-me-downs" then this will probably stretch you a bit--especially if you promised to never allow your children to do the same.

Think about it like this: your parents probably passed the clothing down because they didn't have the money to buy new clothing for each child. Your goal and motivation is different. It may not be that you don't have the money, but you want to use wisdom to maximize your savings.

wisdom for wealth

Hand-me-downs just make good financial sense.

You must be practical when it comes to kids. Children grow too fast for you to invest major dollars into their wardrobes. Stop trying to give your kids what you didn't have and give them what they need and some of what they want. It could hinder you from progressing financially.

Someone once bought my oldest of three sons a very nice wool cashmere dress coat. It was of such quality that all three of my sons wore the coat and there is a nine year age difference from youngest to oldest.

You may need to separate your emotions or childhood experiences from what makes good financial sense. I store some of their nicer, quality items away for the next child while they are still in good condition. Why spend repeatedly when you have the items already? I've done this without compromising style or quality.

You want to think about this if you're going to purchase an expensive item. We purchased an expensive sports team jacket, knowing that it was of such a quality that all three sons would be able to wear it. The youngest son is wearing it now and it still looks new. It is imperative that you take good care of quality items.

I only have one girl, so she gets off the hook on this although friends have given me nice, used clothing for her and she wears them well. Having four kids, this tip has saved me tremendously through the years.

Your Action Point

29

rewards

Some people don't really have a savings, yet they spend as if there is no tomorrow. I am always seeking to acquire the mentality of the wealthy. If it's a principle or habit that works, then I'm going to work it into my financial life.

I once heard a wealthy person say that he uses credit cards which offer rewards so that he can save on travel expenses. That's a sure way to maintain wealth, fostering a "saver's mentality."

wisdom for wealth

Work the system and save.

I have a rewards program on my credit card that I primarily use for my business. I'm going to have many of those expenses anyway, so why not reap the rewards. When I first got the card, I didn't know its value. I noticed the points in the corner of my statement, but never paid attention to how they could be used to my advantage. Then, one day I investigated the program and found that I could save in many ways especially on my flights. To my surprise, I had already earned enough points to receive two gift certificates of my choice. I gave them away as presents at two baby showers that I attended. They made extraordinarily nice gifts and didn't cost me any out-of-pocket expense. Make sure you're not just spending for the rewards; buy what you need.

Currently, I have saved enough points for a free flight. The knowledge of the savings that rewards cards can afford has motivated me because I found a new way to save.

Most, if not all, of the airlines have rewards programs called "Frequent Flyer." This is good because you get points for miles that you are going to travel anyway. My husband saved about $1,000 with a free flight to Hawaii and now has enough points for free travel anywhere in the world. What a deal! Call the airlines that you travel the most and sign up for their frequent flyer program. They will send you a card and when you make your flight arrangements give them your frequent flyer number and they'll give you points based on distance traveled.

Warning: if you are going to redeem your frequent flyer miles, make your reservations well in advance, at least six to nine months, to ensure availability.

Your Action Point

30

---

avoid late fees

*L*ate fees are major business; therefore, you need to make it your business not to incur them. Many institutions are literally banking on receiving late payments. In other words, it can add hundreds of thousands, if not millions of dollars each year to their profit margins. Credit card companies can charge up to $39 or more per late payment. Such fees are literally burying consumers in their debt.

According to an article entitled, "Credit Card Penalties, Fees Bury Debtors" by Cathleen Day and Caroline E. Mayer (Washington Post, Sunday, March 6, 2005), p. A01. One woman's credit card debt doubled in two years simply due to penalties and late fees. What makes it worse is that she hadn't even used the cards at all in two years. Tardiness on her payment triggered late fees being accessed which ultimately caused her interest rate to double. The additional costs that she then incurred, due to the higher interest rate, pushed her over her credit limit. Consequently, the credit card companies added even more penalties. This is a win-lose situation. The creditors win, while the consumer loses. That woman ended up filing for bankruptcy. It was nearly impossible for her to dig herself out of that hole, even though she was working two jobs trying to meet her financial obligations. This is an every day occurrence for many consumers caught in the credit system.

Consumers are seldom shown mercy by having fees waived even if being late was due to unforeseen circumstances, though it certainly won't hurt you to ask. Depending on the situation, they may waive the fee for you once. I understand that making payments to creditors on time is the sole responsibility of the debtor. Since your creditors won't help you, you need to help yourself by deciding to pay on time.

wisdom for wealth

View all late fees and penalties as enemies to financial strength.

Every financial institution or business transaction is subject to fees or penalties for poor money managers or people who experience financial difficulty. They can exploit your weakness by penalizing you for such behavior. Banks, credit agencies, IRS, mortgage companies, auto companies, insurance companies, and even utility companies all charge late fees and penalties. Beware, because late fees and penalties add up quickly, as I just described, if you are habitually late. Having late fees accessed to your accounts should be an eye opener. It indicates that you're in over your head in debt. First, make a mental adjustment with determination to change your financial habits. You must have the mentality that it's not okay to give money away to creditors. Second, restructure your finances to make sure that accounts that could have fees attached are priority and are paid on time. Last, avoid late fees and reward yourself by saving the money that you were losing.

Your Action Point

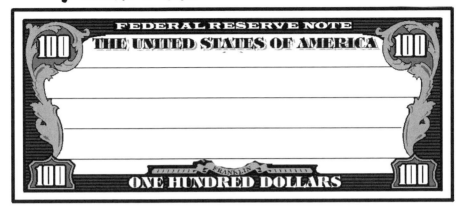

31

refinance only when it increases your financial position

*R*efinancing can yield significant savings even if you do an option arm as opposed to a fixed rate. You can use refinancing as an opportunity to pay your principle down, and this saves in the overall amount of interest that you are paying long term. I refinanced my home mortgage and continued to pay the same amount that I had been paying previously. It reduced my principle about $18,000 over a three year period.

You may ask, "When should I refinance?" In my opinion, when the rates are low enough for you to realize a savings and when you do the math and find that you are going to save more than you spend in refinance fees. For example, if you are selling your home in a year, then the refinance cost may exceed your savings. Your monthly payment may be lower, but given the timeframe, you may not have the chance to break even by recovering your closing costs.

wisdom for wealth

Refinance when it increases your savings.

I would not recommend refinancing to use the equity in your home for debt consolidation. You may or may not be saving when looking at your total financial picture. The consolidating of debt is not the elimination of debt.

This is what I want you to consider from my one-time experience with refinancing for debt consolidation: I had a lower payment, but it did not impact my spending habits. Refinancing seemed to offer short-term relief, but I ended up in a deeper hole by somehow getting back into debt. The worst part was that I lost a portion of the equity in my home which set me back financially.

Think about it, you are borrowing money from your future to pay for debt from your past. You are literally going backwards financially. Does that make good financial sense? You have to answer that question for yourself. Your payment is lower because the debt is stretched out over a longer period. People are in their current situations mainly due to poor money management and with this kind of refinancing, they now have more disposable income to mismanage.

Loss of equity to eliminate debt can put you in a weaker financial position. When you really need the equity it won't be there. Borrowing equity to invest in a safe savings vehicle that would earn you more money is smart. I paid a serious price for this wisdom.

Your Action Point

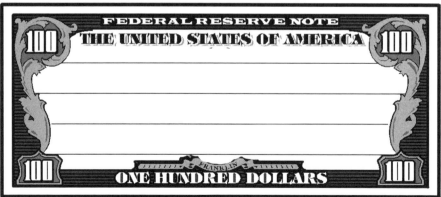

32

a line of credit versus a home equity loan

J previously thought that a line of credit was a brilliant idea for me. I had investment properties and it seemed better to get a line of credit than a mortgage. Years later, I found myself wishing I had never heard of a line of credit.

Lines of credit seem convenient, but remember that convenience costs. If I had it to do all over again, I would have preserved the equity in my investment. It's like paying to borrow your own money when the investment is paid in full. I can't even remember what I did with the money that I got from the line of credit. I'm sure that it was something that I thought made sense at the time.

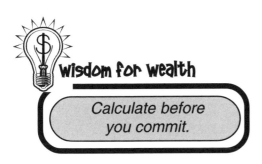

wisdom for wealth

Calculate before you commit.

In the end, the money will be gone and so will your equity. That's not all. The sting of a line of credit is the interest payment. If you get a line of credit and invest the money in a savings vehicle that's earning you more than it's costing in interest, then that makes good financial sense.

You may save more, by having a lower monthly payment, with a line of credit versus a home equity loan. The lower payments may help with cashflow, but you will be paying interest only. So, if it's a long-term situation you will need to pay extra in order to pay down the principle. The interest rate on a line of credit fluctuates based on the prime lending rate. Home equity loans are usually fixed. Make sure that you compare the two.

Your*A*ction *P*oint

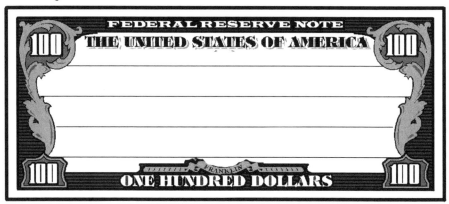

33

a golden rule: "know yourself"

I am a student of life, a life-long learner. Although I help many people in my profession, I spend a lot of time working on myself. I consistently evaluate and reexamine my strengths and weaknesses. This practice gives me a keen awareness of who I am. It also applies to my financial life.

Knowing yourself can save you a lot of money. If you know that money in your hand is like holding on to the wind, then create a system of restraint. You can minimize the cash that you withdraw. You can stop using the ATM! Stay away from the mall. Don't even think about the dollar store.

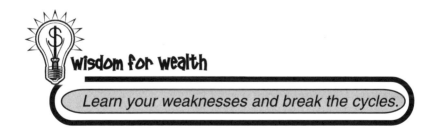

wisdom for wealth

Learn your weaknesses and break the cycles.

Have foreknowledge about your savings account's number one enemy--you. Know your weaknesses and implement a financial structure that compensates for your weaknesses. I know that if I physically went to the bank and cashed my check every week I would spend a lot more money.

Direct deposit allows me to have already sent out my bill money and I literally get what's left. If your entire check is free to be spent at your discretion, then that's different. Turn your weaknesses into strengths and save. Practice makes perfect.

Your*A*ction *P*oint

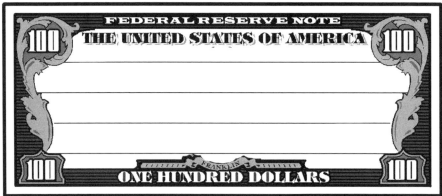

34

---

the deal on cell phones

A friend asked me, "Do you think that you can go without using your cell phone for an entire day?" I thought about it for a moment. My response was that I certainly could if I had to do it. In her opinion, cell phones weren't really a necessity. They're a luxury and a convenience item.

I am able to accomplish a lot while on the go while using my cell phone. Because I have taken care of my business via cell phone, when I get home, I can spend quality time with family without as many phone interruptions.

wisdom for wealth

Use the convenience of a cell phone wisely.

Convenient? Yes, but so are computers, airplanes, and the Internet. What did we do before them? We made do with what we had, but times have changed. For example, instead of driving twenty hours to Florida, I can get there in less than two if I fly. The down side of convenience is that convenience costs. Cell phones are no exception to this rule.

If you feel that a cell phone is a necessity for you, then find the most economical program. Select a package that fits your budget and then use your cell phone accordingly. For instance, if your plan allows you to have unlimited minutes during certain hours, then wait to make your long social calls on your cell phone carrier's dime. Remember, a cell phone is an expense.

Compare companies and their phone-to-phone package and see which one causes you to come out on top. Ask about free incoming calls. Make certain that your after hours calls are free. Pay the minimal additional fee (if applicable) to talk to others who are with the same company. I only pay five dollars extra per month to speak with anyone who is with my same carrier.

The bottom-line is don't blow your savings for a cell phone!

Your Action Point

35

axe the tax

A key way to save money is to properly structure your income to minimize income tax. "Recognize that a $5000 refund means that you loaned the federal government $5000 of your money--interest free--for the year," says Tax Consultant, Lisa Banks. That's about $417 per month. Would that pay a bill for you? If you instead put that $417 a month in a 4% interest-bearing account you would reap an extra $96 for the year, or using it to pay down an 18% loan would save an extra $438 a month in interest, not to mention your debt has decreased significantly. Check with your tax professional to determine how to restructure your withholdings. He or she can advise you concerning what you need to claim in order to keep your money in your pocket.

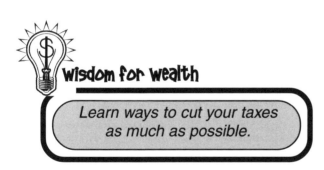

wisdom for wealth

Learn ways to cut your taxes as much as possible.

"Rapid refunds are a rip-off!" says Banks. Remember that the next time you pay an additional $500 for this expensive two week loan. "Most rapid refund customers do not realize that electronic filing will get your money back in two weeks anyhow. This exorbitant fee for getting your refund back two weeks earlier calculates to interest rates from 200% to over 1500% depending upon which rapid refund 'loan shark' you pay," Banks added. "The sad fact, as is usually the case with rip-offs of this nature, is that they are typically targeted to those who can least afford to pay it--the low income who are expecting to receive thousands back in Earned Income Tax Credits," comments Lisa Banks.

Banks also advises, "Medical expenses are not normally high enough to write-off because only the portion that exceeds 10% of your Adjusted Gross Income can be written off; however, there is another way. If your employer offers a flexible spending plan, sign up and have him deduct your estimated medical benefits, pre-tax, from your paycheck. When you incur the expense, submit the receipt and get a reimbursement from your spending account. Be sure not to overestimate, because it is almost always a use it or lose it policy. New policy changes do allow you to use the money for an extra 2.5 months after the close of the year, but after that you forfeit the account balance. If it is a year where you anticipate braces for your child or other major medical expenses, this is a great way to avoid taxes on that portion of your income."

Wondering which of your savings vehicles to pull from to pay for college expenses for you, your spouse, child, stepchild or grandchild? Lisa Banks recommends that you try an IRA. "Normally premature distributions from an IRA are penalized 10% in addition to being added as income to your tax return for the year. You avoid the 10% penalty if the proceeds are used for the cost of tuition, room and board, fees, books and supplies for students enrolled as at least half-time students. These expenses must be incurred in the year of the withdrawal which means you cannot withdraw without penalty to payoff student loans," Banks said.

Your*A*ction *P*oint

Part II

Debt Reduction

36

avoid the trap

*C*redit cards are marketed as prestigious--symbols of status--as if by possessing certain cards you have "arrived." After slipping in and out of debt I finally learned the best usage of credit cards. They are for convenience, but they should not be used as if they were a bank account with cash readily available. I wasn't conscious of the fact that every time I made a credit card purchase I was borrowing money at a very high interest rate and going into debt. The deception is that you don't feel any pain at the point of purchase.

Think about this: if you make only the minimum payment on multiple credit cards, it's probably due to a cashflow crunch. You will make very little progress toward getting out of debt because you'll pay very little on the principle. This results in the consumption of your disposable income on paying credit card interest. In this scenario, you could pay on your cards for an entire year and at the

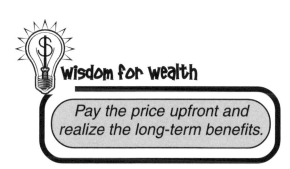

wisdom for wealth

Pay the price upfront and realize the long-term benefits.

end of the year owe the same amount of money or more. I've seen it happen. If you fall into this scenario, you must begin to look at credit card debt as an enemy to your financial goals.

Generally, people charge nonessential items which add up at an amazing rate. Most people are surprised that their balance is so high when they receive their statement. Without knowing it, you could be thousands of dollars in credit card debt and not have the disposable income to just pay it off. This is the trap! Now you are in a long-term commitment to your creditors.

There have been years when I've even paid thousands of dollars in interest on credit cards. I was blind-sided by my purchasing power and had not really counted up the cost of using credit. I realize now that if I would have had a different purchasing strategy and avoided the interest I could have put those thousands in savings. I didn't realize the degree to which credit cards were robbing me of my savings!

You may think that you don't have much money to save. If you use a different purchasing strategy, avoid interest and pay yourself what you would have paid in interest, then there's your money for savings. It took years for me to see that having a credit card really has the potential to be good or bad; depending on how it's used.

If you keep an outstanding balance on the card, then each month that you hold the balance you are getting charged interest. In other words, you are automatically paying much more for the item that you purchased. In addition, it could be an indication that the purchase was made in bad timing because more than likely you "really" didn't have the money for the purchase. If you keep the balance long-term, with just paying the minimum payment, you may never and I mean never get out of the trap!

Your Action Point

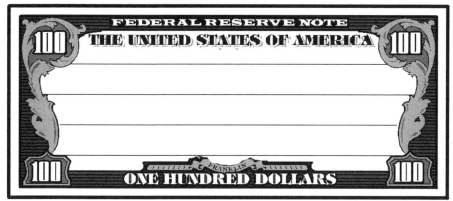

FEDERAL RESERVE NOTE
THE UNITED STATES OF AMERICA
100   100
100   ONE HUNDRED DOLLARS   100
FRANKLIN

37

---

charging
the smart way

One year, I calculated the amount of interest I was paying on credit cards and was floored. Even a low interest rate means very little if you don't pay the card off within 19-22 days of your purchase. If you keep a running balance on your charge card, then you could potentially pay for items several times over. This absolutely cancels out what you originally saved on the "good deal."

I have counseled young college students, who may have been a little down because of their lack of possessions, about their finances. I told them that they were blessed because they didn't have debt and they could start on the right track without being burdened down with the load of debt.

There's a way to charge and avoid the damage that interest does to your savings. Try using a debit card or a Green Dot Visa or Master Card, these are available at your local pharmacy. You can load money on the cards and use them for whatever you wish to purchase. When the money you put on them is gone, then your purchasing power is gone. This allows you to take advantage of the convenience of credit cards without borrowing money and going into debt. Every time that you use a regular credit card you are borrowing money, which is the opposite of saving.

Credit cards are for convenience, but vendors make it convenient for you to borrow instead of save. You have to structure your purchases to protect your goals to save. Look at it; you're spending money that you may not have at the time, buying things that you may not need and paying more than you may realize. If you think about a credit card purchase from the perspective of whether or not you would be able to pay off the card within 30 days (to avoid interest) it may help you to decide whether or not it's a good purchase.

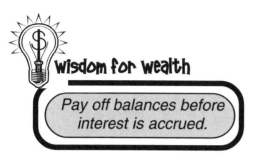

wisdom for wealth

Pay off balances before interest is accrued.

When I saw what those credit card purchases were really costing me, I was driven to come out of that system. I realized that no purchase that I made with credit cards was worth the real price that I paid to have the items. It was weakening my financial position because the interest was stealing the savings and then some.

Your*A*ction *P*oint

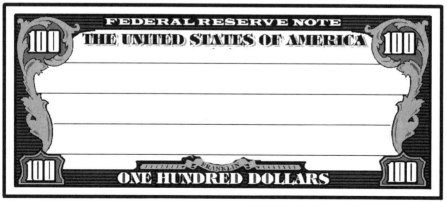

38

Use an "all cash" system

J've read countless books about finances, all of which were helpful in providing a piece to the puzzle on successful money management. One such book talked about living on an "all cash" system. This is where you divide your disposable income, your available spending money, into different categories thus setting your spending parameters. When the cash in that category is spent, then you're done. This will make you pay attention to your spending or cause embarrassment in the checkout line at the grocery store.

It is said that an "all cash" system helps you to save. There was a testimonial in the book about a guy who didn't believe that an "all cash" system would work for him, so he and his wife tried it for a year. When he went to the store he only had the amount of money on him that was allotted, so he couldn't overspend. They completely stopped using credit cards.

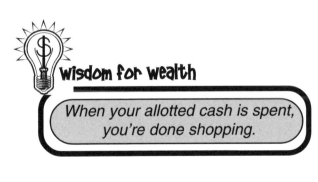

wisdom for wealth

When your allotted cash is spent, you're done shopping.

To their surprise, they had realized a 25 percent savings at the end of the year; that is significant savings. If their net income was $30,000 that year; they saved $7,500 just by implementing this strategy. That is a conservative estimate.

With a checkbook or credit cards it's easy to override the voice of wisdom and make ill-advised or untimely purchases. I have found that the "all cash" system works best with variable expenses like gas, groceries, entertainment, and allowance. It is very good for developing discipline in spending.

Before determining how much money needs to go into a category, make sure that you come up with an accurate figure of how much you really need. You can actually put the allotted money in envelopes labeled according to categories. This system may seem extreme, but it is one of the quickest and most effective ways to maximize your savings by getting a handle on your spending.

Your Action Point

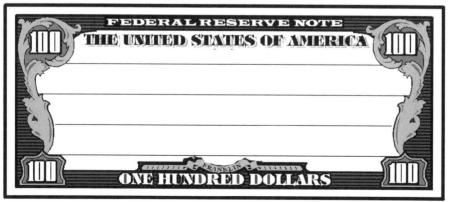

39

---

downsize

*C*ompanies that want to maintain a profitable business sometimes have to make tough choices associated with downsizing. In order to stay in business they must remain profitable, even if it requires some tough cuts or cutbacks.

When you transfer the same mentality into your personal financial life, it may require that you make some tough decisions as well. It's wise to periodically take a close look at how you might downsize for a season to meet your savings goal.

Sometimes a good strategy is to decrease in order to experience increase. I am particularly referring to services or expenses that are probably needed and that you've come to rely on, but you really can't afford. This may include cleaning services, lawn care, cooking services, luxury vehicles, certain "toys" of life and the like. It may be tough because you have hired people to solve those problems in your life or you may have become accustomed to "living large" or on a certain level. The question that you must ask yourself is, "Is this a wise use of my income at this time?" If your answer is, "No" then downsize.

When I reflect on some of the purchases that I have made, they felt good at the time of purchase, but I now realize that they really ended up financially hurting me. There is a principle that says, "expenses increase as income increases." The key is to allow your income to increase without eating up your increase with additional expenses. Living beneath your budget or "downsizing" will free extra cash for savings.

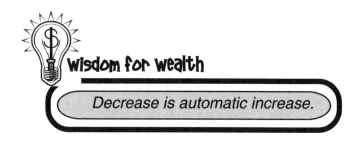

wisdom for wealth

Decrease is automatic increase.

Your Action Point

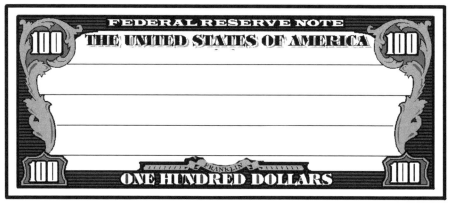

40

credit rating

A good credit rating can save you a ton of money. The interest rate that you pay on large, financed purchases is based on your credit score. The lender determines the interest rate that you are charged by evaluating the level of risk that you present as a borrower. In most cases, this is solely

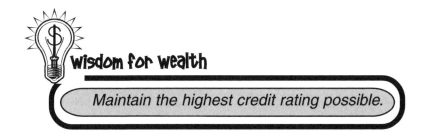

wisdom for wealth

Maintain the highest credit rating possible.

established by your credit score or rating. Almost all lending institutions are automated; they are just looking at the numbers. This is why they can tell you in a few minutes whether or not you are approved.

I've learned in shopping for auto insurance that some auto insurance companies even determine insurance rates based on credit scores. An agent told my husband that people who have lower credit scores are more likely to have an accident. My husband absolutely couldn't understand their justification for this. This philosophy somehow justifies their raising a person's premium based solely on his or her credit scores. In my opinion, the insurance companies just found a way to get more money. What does money management have to do with driving ability? This system is automatically prejudging people. We may think that this is absurd, yet it is the current-day reality. In this scenario a lower score could cost you an additional $500 a year depending on what type of vehicle that you drive.

On mortgages, lenders have offered rates as low as 1.5 percent to individuals with credit scores that were approximately 620 or higher. One individual who secured this low rate saved more than $1,500 a month on his mortgage payment. That equals $18,000 a year just because of his credit score. Over three years, he would realize a savings of $54,000. So, before you finance a major purchase you need to search for a credit repair expert. One such source is www.trinitylenders.com. You can go to this website and click "credit update."

Two individuals with comparable incomes, but drastically different credit scores went to lease the same vehicle. One paid $209 per month, while the other paid $460. This is a difference of $251 per month, totaling $3,012 per year.

These same two individuals went to take advantage of a 12 month $99 a month lease special for a full size SUV. The one with the higher credit score was approved over the phone. The one with the lower credit score was required to submit so much information that he became discouraged and chose not to do it.

There are numerous real life examples to substantiate the savings experienced with higher credit scores, so raise your score and soar!

Your*A*ction *P*oint

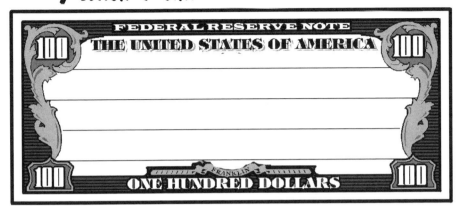

41

Just say, "no!" to no payment, no interest

Delaying payment is an enticing way to shop. You can continuously spend and not pay for your purchase until later, much later. "No Payment, No Interest" advertisements are common and effective. Every day they draw unsuspecting victims into their lair. The question that you need to ask yourself is, "If I can't afford it now, will I be able to afford it later?" Trust me, the answer is typically, "No" and you will have to pay dearly if the balance isn't paid when the time is up. All of the interest that you were supposed to save on the deal will be added back into the balance.

wisdom for wealth

Pay without delay.

The problem is that they allow you to make the purchase without the cost of the item impacting your budget. All the while, if you continue to function as if you haven't made the purchase, then when it comes time to pay the full balance you are unprepared. If you're disciplined enough to be prepared when it comes time to pay, then you're disciplined enough to avoid using this method to purchase.

"No Payment, No Interest" sales are deceptive. It feels like you're getting something for nothing, but you're not! When you receive that first monthly statement, pay it immediately, don't delay! Sooner or later your time will be up and you will have to pay the full amount of the bill or endure the added interest which of course, defeats your original purpose of taking advantage of no interest.

"No Payment, No Interest" is a win-lose situation. If you factor in a repayment schedule, then you won't get caught off guard, and you win. If you do get caught off guard and get the interest added back in, then they win and you lose.

Your *A*ction *P*oint

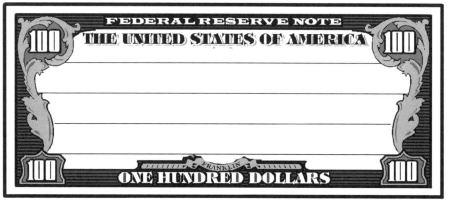

42

it is in your best interest not to pay interest

It's in your best interest not to pay interest! It is in your best interest to gain interest! I don't know if I've seen or experienced anything else that can rob you of financial strength more effectively and quickly than interest.

Give yourself an "Interest Test" by adding up all of your interest-bearing accounts and see just how much you are paying to use your creditor's money. Add your car loan, mortgage, credit cards, any lines of credit or home equity loans, and the like. Do the calculations based on what you are paying yearly in interest. It may be the surprise of your life or just an eye opener.

wisdom for wealth

It's in your best interest not to pay interest.

On most large purchases like a home or car, many people don't have the money to pay cash. This needs to get your attention. It seems as if we aren't left any options other than paying interest. It's the way of the world. As soon as you are able, work your way out of the interest system because it's not in your best interest.

You could be losing some $20,000 a year or more, as I discovered. Being indebted for five years can cost you $100,000 in interest! You will recognize that you, the borrower, are certainly now servant to the lender.

Sometimes the asset can outweigh the interest. For instance, if the interest is on an investment and you're generating income to offset it, then that is not really costing you because someone else is paying the interest. Just follow what makes sense for you. Consider certain kinds of interest as an enemy to financial freedom. In my opinion, the only kind of interest that is not an enemy is interest paid on an income-producing investment such as a mortgage on rental property where the rental income is twice the mortgage payment, for example.

If you must pay interest, then for sure shop around for the best interest rates. The bottom-line is that you want to pay as little interest as possible even on investments because that is more money that can be saved. Money stretches a lot further when interest is not involved.

Your*A*ction *P*oint

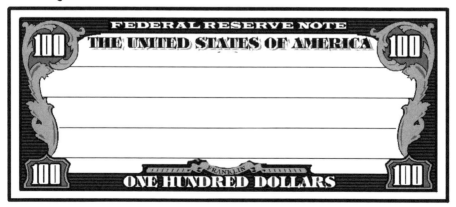

Part III

Budgeting

43

---

live by a budget

Some may feel as though they don't make enough money to justify budgeting. Others consider maintaining a budget as too much of a hassle. I believe that all income needs to be guided by a budget. It lets you know where you are headed and whether you're on the right course. Most importantly, it lets you know what money you really have to spend at any given time.

I would like to illustrate this by using driving as an example. When you get into a vehicle, you probably don't just drive aimlessly. Generally, when you drive it's because you need to go somewhere specific. It is essential to have directions if you ever plan to reach your destination. If it's a familiar destination, then you're set; however, when it is some place that you've never been, then you need accurate, detailed directions that will guide you along the best course. In the same way, a budget provides directions that guide you to your successful financial future. If your destination is "financial freedom," then your budget is the road map to getting there. You don't have to play a guessing game, take wrong turns, or end up on a dead end street.

A budget guides your spending like a road map guides a driver. It lets you know when you're off course and when you're on course.

Yes, it takes time to create and manage a budget, but it saves money when you live by it.

wisdom for wealth

Your budget is the road map to financial success.

A budget lets you know your starting point. If you were lost and called OnStar for assistance, the agent would first locate you and then accurately guide you to your destination. Once you know financially where you are, by utilizing the help of a budget, your journey should be a lot clearer and your savings plan a lot closer.

Your *Action Point*

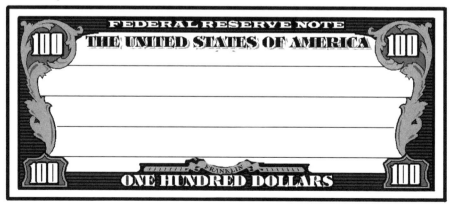

FEDERAL RESERVE NOTE
THE UNITED STATES OF AMERICA
100 100
100 100
FRANKLIN
ONE HUNDRED DOLLARS

44

work your plan

It's one thing to lay out a budget and a totally different thing to successfully maintain it. Having a budget is half of the battle. Following a budget takes additional skill and pure determination!

A principle about money management that I recently adopted from a financial conference Is this: one should manage money every day for at least 20-30 minutes. Previously, I looked at my budget once or twice a week, mainly in time to send out bills. I've since changed that. I lay out the plan far enough to see what really lies ahead and I study it daily.

wisdom for wealth

The disciplined person plans the work and then works the plan.

Daily financial management is sharpening my money management skills. I am on top of things instead of under circumstances. I have a greater sense of control. My budget controls my choices. I was losing a lot of money because my spending wasn't lining up with my budget. By managing my money daily, I am constantly aware of areas where I may need to make adjustments to meet my financial goals. Before I started daily managing, I would often be lost, even though I thought I was budgeting.

Study your budget daily. This practice allows you to keep your finger on the pulse of your financial life. In doing so, constantly evaluate where you can save. Stay on course.

Your*A*ction *P*oint

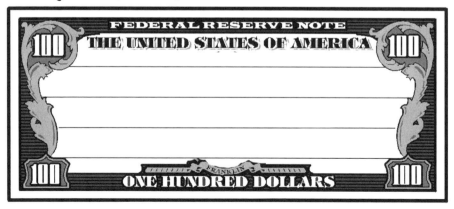

45

---

stay balanced

Keeping a checkbook balanced seems simple, but it's not as easy as it looks especially if you don't necessarily have the skills of an accountant. Use of ATM's can make balancing even more challenging. I've also found that at times when I was extremely busy I neglected to make the entries along the way and that was costly. When you don't make timely entries, you write your checks based on a mental estimation of your balance. With so many charges against your checking account it is virtually impossible to keep track of your balance mentally.

I am absolutely amazed at how I graduated with high distinction from high school, excelled in college, and still fell short of the "life skills" needed for financial success. I don't think I'm alone in this category. I didn't even have a checking account until I was a college graduate. It has taken years to acquire these skills in the midst of life's every day demands.

wisdom for wealth

No pain--no gain. Take the time, and the "pain" to keep your checkbook balanced.

Here are some practical tips on balancing your checkbook: don't forget to record monthly automatic withdrawals immediately; record your checks soon after they are written; and use a calculator, adding machine or budgeting software to ensure that your math is correct. Once, I made a subtraction error which caused my balance to be off by $1,000. I was certainly glad to catch it in time. Of course, I now go over my figures with a calculator to ensure accuracy.

It is also good to have an overdraft protection on your account as a safety net, but it doesn't replace balancing because you are still charged for overdrafts. The check may be covered in order for you so save face, but not without a cost.

The best thing to do is to find a quality computer program, like Quicken, to help with money management. Put in the facts and let the computer do the balancing act.

Your*A*ction *P*oint

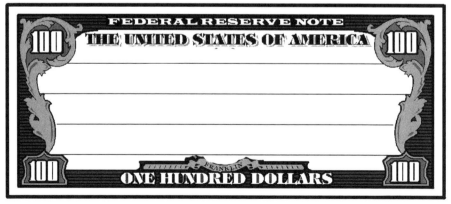

46

organize your life and slow down

Several times I found myself in an unusually busy season in my life. In looking back, I see that I was attempting to juggle too many things at once. This fast-pace lifestyle resulted in disorder in several areas of my life, but I felt the greatest impact financially. I discovered that I spend a lot more money when my sense of order is disturbed. I have figured out that *disorder is costly*.

If you consistently live with disorder, then your financial life will reflect the same. Chaos occurs when things are done without a plan. I would buy things that I could not find and find things I bought after their period of usefulness had expired. When my life lacks order, I notice that I dine out more often because I don't take time to plan for meals. On the contrary, when I am well organized, I save time and money. Order saves money. When there is order in your life you can operate more efficiently and consequently save more money. I can guarantee that being organized will save you money just as being disorganized will cost you unnecessarily.

This is a sure saver. Sometimes I joke with my friends that it costs me $300 just to leave the house. The fact is that living costs. The hustle and bustle of life is expensive. I just experienced the heaviest travel season of my life and can say for sure that it costs more to live on the go. My advice is slow down: "Rome wasn't built in a day." On the other hand, if your lifestyle demands hustle and bustle, then travel with maximum savings in mind. Make the least expensive travel arrangements.

Once I had what I thought was a brilliant idea. I decided to let my kids plan the family activities. They were so excited, but by the end of the day, I was not. I had spent nearly $300. Gas costs were $60 just to get on the road. Gas prices are motivation enough for me to consider where I absolutely have to go and what can wait. Motivation is the birthplace of creativity. My children still enjoy activities, I just guide them toward those that don't cost me $300 per day. I think they'd much rather see a healthy inheritance.

We purchased a ping pong table and I was amazed at how much fulfillment my kids get out of learning to play. It keeps them occupied for a while and I don't have to leave my home, so in the end I save again. Count the cost! Organize!

wisdom for wealth

Order your life for maximum savings. Slow down and save!

Your*A*ction *P*oint

47

---

navigate
your errands

J have a natural gift of navigation. In other words, I have a pretty good sense of direction; therefore, every time I leave the house I have a mental plan as to what is the best and most efficient route to take to save on gas and time.

Sometimes I might need to do something that requires me to go on the other side of town. I think about when I actually need it done and if I have other things to do while on that side of town, so that I can get them done all at once. For instance, if I need to go to the mall across town, I determine if there is anything else that I can accomplish that's nearby. After making a mental note of all the things that I can accomplish while in that area, I

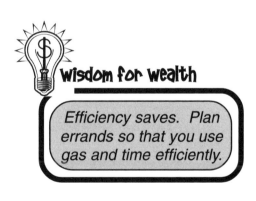

wisdom for wealth

Efficiency saves. Plan errands so that you use gas and time efficiently.

head out to run my errands. If, on the other hand, the trip can wait, I'll plan to take care of it when I'm going that way. I might have seven stops to make in a day. I try to make a complete circle. I think about the best starting point with the ending point that is nearest to my home. This drastically minimizes my gas expense and frees income for savings. What really matters is that at the end of the day I have more time and more money.

Your*A*ction *P*oint

48

cutting gas costs

*T*here are several ways that you can save by cutting your automobile gasoline costs. For instance, you might want to reduce the "lead in your foot" while driving. "Fuel economy suffers at speeds higher than 60 and drops like a stone above 70," says Chris Grundler of the National Vehicle and Fuel Emissions laboratory in Ann Arbor, Michigan.

Check for discounted gas. My husband usually keeps me informed about where to purchase the cheapest gas in town. Nine times out of ten, I fill up at the corner gas station; I have a rewards card at the station. The rewards card affords you savings up to $0.50 off per gallon or $25 worth of gas as you rack up a certain number of points from gas purchases.

wisdom for wealth

Reduce your gas expense by investigation and conservation.

You can go to www.gasbuddy.com, enter your zip code and find the lowest gas prices in your area. If the trip across town to fill up is worth the savings, then it's a wise choice.

My son is so attentive that he figured out what days the service attendant changed the gas prices. He would say, "You need to get your gas today because they're going to change it tonight." Someone also told me that gas prices usually change closer to the weekend or holidays, so I now pay close attention to this in order to realize the savings. There's no way to avoid paying for gas unless you don't use a vehicle. The smart thing to do is to employ strategies that allow you to maximize your savings while you drive.

There are grocery store chains that also have gas stations. They usually offer discounts if you have their rewards card. I have a card that offers a certain amount off gasoline per dollars spent on groceries. That's a win-win situation because I'm going to buy the groceries anyhow. When I fill up my tank and realize significant savings, I'm happy. I may have only saved $10, but it is money that I can keep in my pocket.

I read where low tire pressure can also decrease your gas mileage by 10 percent, so make sure that your tires remain inflated according to what is specified in your owner's manual. Years ago I heard that starting your car consumes a lot of gas; I have since found out that idling your car for more than one minute is like starting it again. In other words, you are consuming more gas just sitting still. Turn your vehicle off when you're sitting there talking to a friend, waiting on a train, or waiting in a long, stagnant line while picking up the kids from school.

Your **A**ction **P**oint

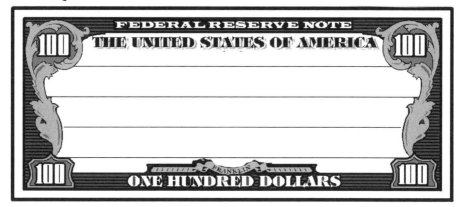

49

low budget recreation

*T*here are free activities in every community, take advantage of them. Basketball Camps, Vacation Bible School, Festivals, Library Programs, or a trip to the park are fun activities that are free.

The goal is to create low budget recreation for your family. An inflatable pool, video rentals and putt-putt golf are fun, inexpen-

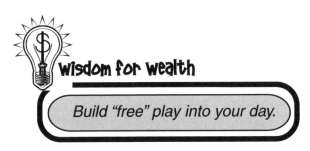

wisdom for wealth

Build "free" play into your day.

sive activities. If you decide to go to the movies instead of renting a video, then find a discount theatre or one that offers rewards (a free movie for every so many tickets purchased). Some discount theatres only cost $2, though you may not be able to view the most popular movie when it is first released. It is a way to save.

I can easily spend $65 for a movie night out with my family as opposed to less than ten dollars to rent several videos with homemade popcorn. Most often, the kids are just happy to spend time with their parents no matter what the cost. If you focus on building a wonderful relationship with your children then they may not remember the movie, but they will remember the time that you spent together. You can accomplish the goal of quality time without it blowing your budget.

Your*A*ction *P*oint

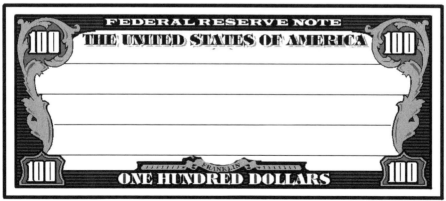

50

conserve, conserve, conserve.

*I*f you've never really paid attention to this word, "conserve," then pay attention. *Conserve* means "to keep or guard, to hold." This paints a good word picture as it relates to savings. Conserving allows you to keep or guard your money, which allows you to hold on to the money that you earn.

When I wash a full load of laundry instead of a half load, I'm conserving. When I wait until the dishwasher is full to wash the dishes, I'm conserving. When I turn out "all" of the lights in my home that aren't being used, I'm conserving. When I un-plug all of the electrical items that aren't being used, I'm conserving. I'm using less and in turn holding on to more savings. All of the resources that I'm conserving have a price tag attached to their use.

wisdom for wealth

Conserve and guard your savings.

There are multiple ways to conserve. I wash a lot of laundry each week, which is probably the same testimony of mothers all over the world. I try to be efficient with the laundry. One day I noticed that I had a lot to wash. I know "a lot" is relative, but I really mean a lot. I started looking for the culprits and I found them to be my four children. They were throwing clean clothes into the dirty laundry basket. I even found new clothes with the tags still on them in the laundry!

I couldn't believe it. I kept thinking that I had just washed something and they hadn't worn it, but it was in the wash again. What I was thinking was right. They may have showered, worn an outfit for a couple of hours and tossed it in the dirty clothes basket. Dirty clothes baskets are for "dirty" clothes! I now have my children hang those clothes up because they can be worn again. In making that adjustment, we were able to conserve water, energy, soap, time, and sanity. Remember, the money that you don't have to spend on excess, you save.

I love Christmas time, especially when I was a kid and since I've had kids. When my kids were really young and didn't know any better, I didn't buy a tree or decorate. Once they began to take notice and ask questions, I gave in. We love to travel through our neighborhood and see all of the beautiful decorations. As I would look, I'd find myself thinking, "That must be costing a lot of money." Well, for the past three years, we've hung lights outside and we have found that you can put them on a timer. They can come on at dusk and go off at daybreak. This saves money, but preserves the season's delight.

Your**A**ction **P**oint

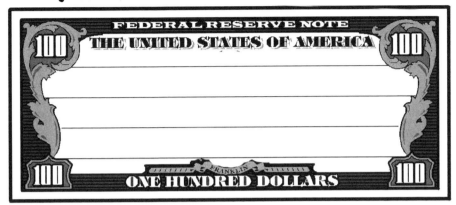

51

---

control the thermostat before it controls you

Not monitoring your thermostat is like giving away your money. I'm not against giving because giving is a good thing. In fact, I'm a generous giver. I'm just not in the habit of giving to the utility monopoly. I like to determine the gift, the amount and the recipients to whom I give. I don't think I'm alone on this--I've yet to run across anyone who likes to give money away to his or her energy company. In fact, most people want a refund.

wisdom for wealth

Controlling your thermostat saves you money.

This is usually an area that we do not think about until we receive our monthly bill or worse yet, we can sometimes feel powerless to change our results. Our energy company does all the calculating, so the cost really seems to be in the company's control. There are some things that we can do to have some say-so in what our energy use is costing us.

You give away money when you leave your thermostat on higher temperatures while you're home. Lowering the thermostat a few degrees can make a difference. Also, by all means turn it down while you're away. No one is using the heat so why overheat your home? All you're doing is keeping the furniture warm. You can have your thermostat on a timer as well and this helps you to only use energy that's necessary or desired.

Seal drafty areas to prevent your heat from escaping. Keep the thermostat on a constant temperature, not excessively hot. If you're hot, then you're probably giving away money. My previous home had two furnaces. I kept the area of the house that was least used at a lower temperature, especially at night, because it was not our sleeping area. Buy well-insulated blankets to keep warm at night.

I religiously turn out all lights that aren't being used and I train my kids likewise. As an adult, I can really understand why my parents attempted to drill this habit into my siblings and me. Of course, we had absolutely no concept of its value then, but we all got a revelation as adults upon having to foot the utility bill. Most of all, don't give money away.

If you can make some adjustments in your habits, you can potentially save hundreds of dollars a year in energy use.

Your Action Point

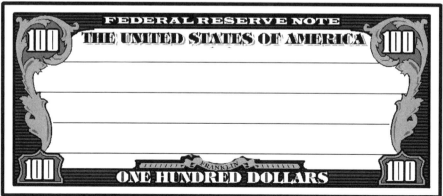

52

energy budget plan

*U*tility budget plans could be a viable savings option for you. The utility company averages your yearly payment and charges you an equal monthly payment throughout the year. Knowing the exact amount of your utility bill could help you tremendously with cashflow management. With the rise and fall of gas prices and temperatures, the fluctuation of your monthly bill can cause you to be on quite a rollercoaster ride.

wisdom for wealth

Protect your budget by alleviating uncontrollable expenses.

For years I resisted getting on a budget plan for gas and utilities, mainly because I didn't want to pay the higher bills during the warmer months. I didn't use nearly as much energy during those months. In retrospect, the lower, consistent winter bill more than balances out the higher summer bill.

After trying the energy budget plan, I found that you really can save. One example of savings was with a rental house where my payment was reduced to $140 a month, even during the winter. I compared that to my previous monthly winter utilities averaging $500. It reduced the winter gas prices by about $360 a month; this is 72 percent!

To sign up for the energy budget plan just call your local utility company and they'll calculate what your bill would be and you do the math! In order to receive the best rate, you need to sign up before April. If you wait until the later part of the year, your plan will be higher due to the upcoming winter months.

Your**A**ction **P**oint

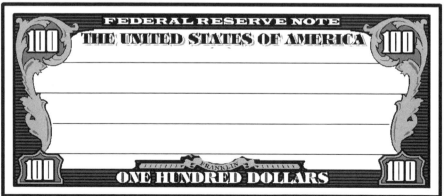

53

double up!
consider a roommate

A roommate can come in handy. When I graduated from college and landed my first job, to my surprise, a college associate had landed one with the same company. We decided to room together since we both were going to the same office every day. Sharing the load saved me a bundle. Think about it, all of our expenses were cut in half; the rent, utilities, groceries and gas (because we car pooled).

Our lives weren't complicated at all and it worked. Within a year I was married, but the time that I was there saved me money. Our starting salaries were about $18,500 a year. That was twenty years ago and after expenses, I didn't have much left. Imagine how the cost of living has increased in twenty years! If doubling up was a good idea then it certainly is now. My husband and I have had people live with us on occasion (free of charge) to help them get established. This saved them tons of money.

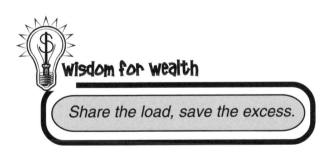

wisdom for wealth

Share the load, save the excess.

When you consider a roommate, you must look at compatibility with regard to personality and domestic habits. Weigh it. If it's a good financial move that would give you some breathing room and the opportunity to advance financially, then share the load.

Your*A*ction *P*oint

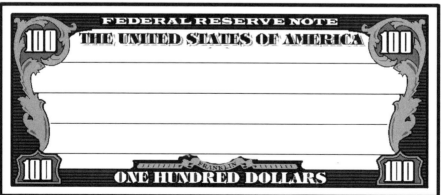

54

plan a menu

*P*lanning a menu actually saves in many ways. When my husband asks, "What's for dinner?" and I don't have a plan, I just want to scream. It strikes a nerve. I pride myself in being a productive person, so to be caught without a plan is torture.

wisdom for wealth

Gain control by budgeting for food with a plan in mind.

I'm not the Betty Crocker-type. When my mother was in the kitchen, I was in the streets playing basketball. When I got married, at the age of 23, I was certainly behind in my culinary skills. To this day, I must admit that cooking is still a sore spot for me. It's not my favorite thing to do and yet it's necessary as a wife and mother.

Menus have saved me much time, money and frustration. There have been times when I've shopped for groceries without a menu and it has seemed as if I could hardly piece a meal together. At other times, I have had clear direction about what I was going to cook for the week and I was able to be very cost efficient. Since food is a major budget item, this expense can be best kept under control by a menu.

I have been guilty of buying certain food without a meal plan in mind, and those foods have gone to waste or sat in my cabinet for months until they were too old to use. A menu would have helped me avoid those wasteful purchases.

Your*Action* *Point*

55

pack the sack

Sack lunches can cost considerably less than eating out. A sack lunch may seem a little "kiddish," but it's frugal. Carrying a sack lunch gives you the advantage of advance planning, which allows you to purchase groceries at a good price.

In the past, I would buy salads every day for lunch which ranged from $3.50 to $7. It was convenient because they were already prepared. Let's use $5 as an average cost for the salads. That means that I spent $25 per week for lettuce! Can I save by preparing my salads at home? You betcha. I now purchase salad fixin's and prepare them at home to the tune of less than $5 per week.

wisdom for wealth

Taking your lunch to work saves money!

Your goal is to realize savings wherever possible. I have a friend who recently made this same adjustment. She and her husband both purchased their lunch every day. They now both take sack lunches to work daily. She informed me that as a result she has identified $50 a week that she is able to save. She followed my advice and opened a separate savings account that she faithfully deposits that $50 into weekly. Previously, she stated that she couldn't find any money to save. Fifty dollars a week equals $2600 a year without interest.

Your**A**ction **P**oint

56

look it up!

We're in a generation of convenience seekers. We're consumed by our need for speed. Everything has to be quick and at our fingertips or it's considered prehistoric. Speed and convenience are wonderful things, but the cost often overshadows the true value. A lot of things are just matters of conditioning. I have sat within eyeshot of a phonebook and called Directory Assistance to get a number that was in the book.

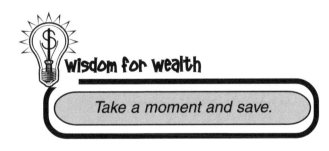

wisdom for wealth

Take a moment and save.

Every time that you use Directory Assistance it costs upwards of two dollars. It may not seem like much, but over a period of a month it can add up. The issue is that this is more often than not an avoidable expense if you are willing to let your fingers do the walking.

My cell phone carrier also offers Directory Assistance. It's a great feature when you're on the go and you need a number in a pinch.

That pinch is really a bite out of your wallet. My cell phone plan charges $1.95 per directory assisted call. Imagine how much it costs on a yearly basis to regularly use this service.

Convenience is a powerful temptation, but it's better to resist and create a system that works for you, saving time and money. Store frequently used phone numbers in your cell phone. If the call is not urgent, then wait until you can look up the number. Look up the phone numbers of businesses that are on your errand list before you leave home. Create an address book with important phone numbers at your fingertips.

Do whatever you can to save money. Don't just give money away. A good rule of thumb: if it's not an emergency, it can wait.

Your*A*ction *P*oint

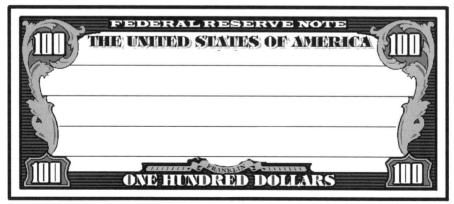

57

bulk up

*B*uying in bulk is a good way to save. Businesses do it all of the time. If you look at your household as a business, then buying in bulk makes dollars and sense. It saves money because you're not sending your most valuable employee (you) on errands when you run out of the insignificant, significant stuff. It also saves money on a per unit basis because you're paying less per unit, for more units. In addition, it saves money because you're not burning gas running back and forth to your local store for staple items.

wisdom for wealth

Buy more, spend less.

Have you ever heard the expression "time is money"? It's true. You cannot afford to have your time swallowed up because you keep running out of things and you've got to go back to the store. If you were the CEO of a major corporation, would you send your most productive and valuable executive to the corner store for jellybeans several times a week? Of course not. You'd want that person in his or her creative flow, pumping out ideas to make the business more profitable. This principle is practical only if you are consuming the amount that you are purchasing in bulk: if not, then your bulk purchase ends up being a waste. Buy in bulk based on need and use.

Your**A**ction **P**oint

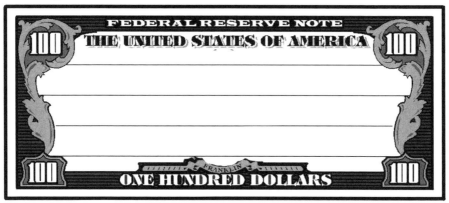

58

---

get on track

I mentioned this earlier, but I would like to expound on this savings strategy. Tracking your spending is a powerful tool for the revelation of your overall spending habits. It is also essential for budgeting. You can't really have an accurate budget until you have a pretty good idea of how much should be allotted for various expenses. A budget simply allows you to execute a plan, but the plan should be true to your reality or it will be hard to manage.

Allow 30 to 60 days of tracking to get a pretty good feel for how much you are actually spending. If you spend the least amount, let's say, one dollar on gum, then write it down in your tracking log. For instance, I would write down $150 per week for groceries in my budget, but when I really thought about it, I didn't know how I came up with that figure. My thought process was, "$150 should be enough to spend per week." Consequently, I would exceed that amount every week. I never really had any idea of what I was spending in groceries until I tracked my spending for 30 days. Before I actually tracked my grocery spending, I would go to the store and write a check. When the food ran out, I would go back to the store and write another check. One quick way to calculate your grocery expense within 30 days is to keep your receipts. Receipts give a clear picture of what you're spending. Once you've calculated your spending habits then you can accurately budget.

Tracking your spending helps you to identify the frivolous, hidden expenses that can be eliminated for savings. This, along with arming yourself with an accurate budget, can make you a highly skilled saver.

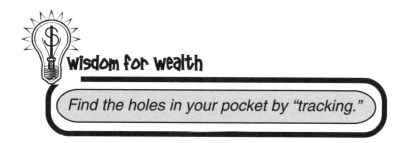

wisdom for wealth

Find the holes in your pocket by "tracking."

Your*A*ction *P*oint

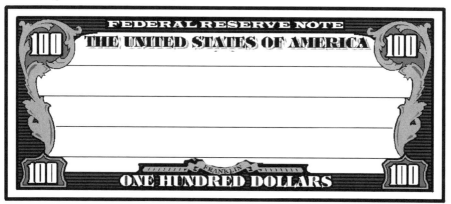

59

resist your "snack attack"

When I was a kid, I loved the corner store in my neighborhood. I called it the candy store. Eating snacks is an acquired habit. It often begins when you're a child. The "snack attack" is costly in several ways, but for the sake of our subject, let's stick with money. Snacks add up quickly.

When I first got married, my husband and I went to a financial advisor. He suggested that we write down everything that we spent, no matter how small the item. This is pretty common advice in order to track your spending, so we did it for 30 days. It was an eye-opener. Overall, we handled our money wisely, but we were amazed at how much we spent on snacks. We usually snacked while at work.

wisdom for wealth

Track the snacks.

Recently, my family started chewing gum. Out of habit, we would just go to the store or gas station and pick up a pack. The only problem is that there are six of us and each person got his or her own pack. We each chewed nearly a pack a day. It cost us $1 per pack times 6! Before I knew it, we were spending $6 every other day for gum. Four packs per person, per week, equals $24 a week for gum. That's $96 a month and $1,344 a year for gum!

Thank God that I stopped early on and did the math. Once I did the math, my kids were instantly delivered from their gum chewing habit. My husband and I still chew gum, but I have since found our favorite gum in bulk and I purchase it while on sale (often for half price).

If you enjoy snacking, then try tracking this habit and see what it's really costing you. Better yet, try eliminating it for a time and see what it's saving you.

Your*A*ction *P*oint

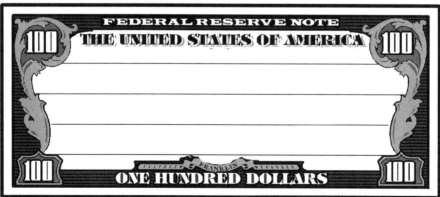

60

eat before you go

ever go to the grocery store on an empty stomach is a warning that I've heard repeatedly over the years. Your wallet will thank you. It's one of the hardest temptations there is to overcome. You'll have to fight off the bakery, the deli, the salad bar and in some stores, the sushi bar. Because you're hungry, before you know it your cart will be full of everything that looks good, which causes you to overspend.

wisdom for wealth

An empty stomach can cause an empty pocket.

When you are shopping and hungry, it can be costly. Eating before you go grocery shopping or taking along a healthy snack will reduce the chances of you overspending. Nuts, fruit, yogurt, protein bars or drinks are all good fill-ins; and the best part is that you probably got them on sale. Satisfying your hunger beforehand is healthier for you financially as well as nutritionally and you accomplish your goal--you save.

Your *Action* *Point*

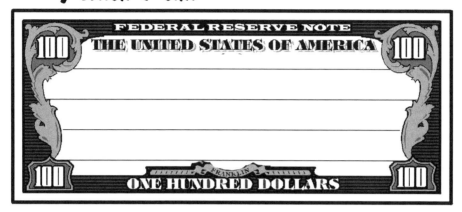

61

---

creative socializing

sually getting together with friends and family involves some level of partaking of food. If you're not careful such socializing can be very costly, though it's a good thing. If guests are coming to your home, then it is proper etiquette to offer them something to eat and or drink. In addition, going out with friends on a regular basis can be very costly.

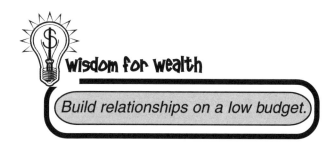

wisdom for wealth

Build relationships on a low budget.

I am a generous person who really likes being a blessing to others, and this often results in my asking for the bill at a dinner when out with friends. Since this is the case, I need to plan for this in my budget and assess what amount is really prudent for me to spend.

Make sure that the money that you spend socializing doesn't consume your savings. Find creative things to do that don't cost you money on a consistent basis. Instead of going out to eat, stay at home and serve light refreshments or have your guests bring a dish to pass. Purchase board games or have your guests bring along their favorite games for entertainment. In this way, you are accomplishing the dual objectives of building relationships and saving at the same time.

Your*A*ction *P*oint

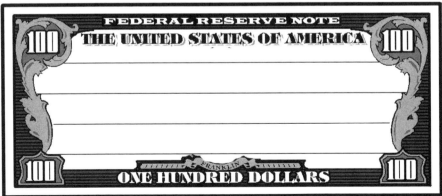

62

two are better than one: car pooling

When I was fresh out of college, I had a roommate. We took turns weekly driving to work. This is not uncommon. Car pool lots are provided for all day parking.

wisdom for wealth

Car pooling: try it, your budget will like it.

Car pooling saves in two ways: purchasing gas and the wear and tear on your vehicle. It also saves on mileage, and this helps the resale value of the vehicle, thus increasing savings.

If you and a coworker are going to the same place, for the same amount of time, and can make it work, then try car pooling and save.

Your *A*ction *P*oint

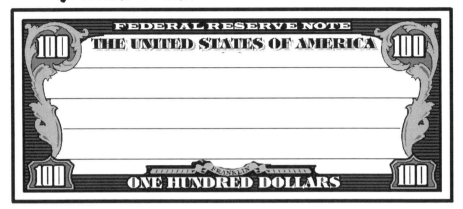

63

when dining out

Who doesn't like to dine out? There's fun, socializing, and best of all you're not doing the dishes! Don't get caught in the moment. Think of ways to save while you dine. My family and I had a great meal and lots of fun at a restaurant. I was glad that we went out until the bill came. I reviewed it and realized that I had spent more than $10 on drinks and almost $15 on appetizers. That is $25 added to my bill which we could have done without.

wisdom for wealth

Have a good time, but at a good price.

After getting the bill we realized that we should have had water and waited for our main course. Besides, water is free and healthier. As a family of six we can easily spend nearly $100 dining out, depending on where we dine. The funny thing about it is that once you get the bill from an "enjoyable" meal, you lose your joy. Another thing that can cost a lot of money is appetizers. Prices on some appetizers rival that of main courses. Do you really need an appetizer? When you consider your savings account, what's another 10-15 minutes waiting for your entrée?

We usually leave a 20 percent tip for the service that we receive. The added expense of drinks and appetizers also increases the amount of the tip.

Don't get tricked, especially if you are really hungry, and order more than you can eat. My parents called it, "your eyes being bigger than your belly."

Your*A*ction *P*oint

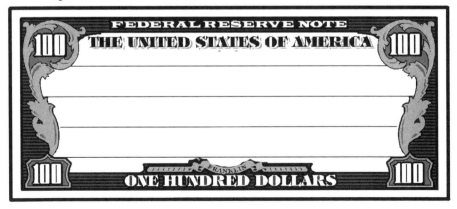

Part IV

Purchasing Strategies

64

let the joneses have one up on you

*O*ver the years I have repeatedly heard the cliché about "keeping up with the Joneses," whoever they may be. In other words, it isn't necessary to compete with your neighbor. Let him have the new boat, new car or new deck. You're also letting him have the new bill.

If what other people have stirs the spender in you then my advice is sweet and simple: "Let the Joneses have one up on you!" Besides, by keeping up with the Joneses you're proclaiming, "I can keep up with your debt and do you one better!" Is that really what you want to communicate?

wisdom for wealth

Don't envy someone else's debt.

I've learned to direct my life based on what's best for my family and me. Other people have their own plans and purposes, so what's good for one person may not be good for another. It may not be a matter of affordability; it may simply be that the timing is not good for you to buy the item. Have you ever considered that you may not need the item at all? Don't feel pressured to have what Texans call "big hat, no cattle." This refers to an outward appearance of success, but no real financial portfolio to substantiate it.

Your*A*ction *P*oint

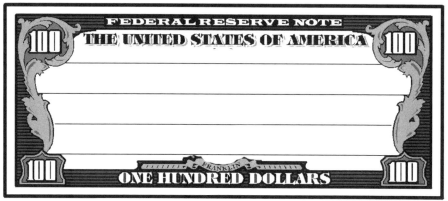

65

---

beware of "impulse buying"

Are you an "impulse shopper?" I am. Or, I should say, I was. I've been motivated by a "silver-tongued" sales person, overwhelmed by a mood, or convinced that "I deserve it" more times than I can count.

When I examined my money habits I saw that the feeling of "missing out" was my problem. I somehow felt as though if I didn't make the purchase, then the opportunity would pass me by. This feeling is often the motivation for ill-advised decisions that seem to fill an immediate need, but cause long-term financial damage. This perspective causes you to spend when you really didn't plan on it. In fact, it was probably "forced into the budget," meaning that you had to "juggle" something to make it happen. Habits like this lead to financial disaster. Unfortunately, you don't really realize it until you regret it.

Impulse buying is often an unconscious, misguided attempt to fulfill some void in the purchaser's life. You may want to do some introspection to discover the root emotion that hides behind the impulse. It's more profitable to discover the root of the emotion that's causing you to become an impulse buyer. In times past, I have caught myself going to spend simply because I was angry. Are you tired? Frustrated? Angry? Hurt? Lonely? Disappointed?

Insecure? Instead of shopping, take some time to address the real issue. If it is not a life or death situation then it can wait for a better day--a day when you can "really" afford the item. Besides, if you wait a while the price will probably drop.

I've learned to negotiate the purchase or simply walk away. It's not a bad thing to do; in fact, it is a very good thing to do. Salespeople and marketers try to convince you that you can't live without the item, but I find that the more I walk away, the better I live.

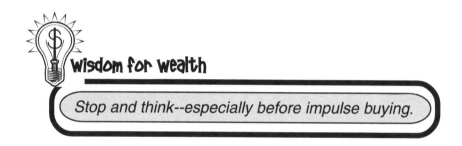

wisdom for wealth

Stop and think--especially before impulse buying.

Your**A**ction **P**oint

66

"going out of business" sales

A failed business is nothing to rejoice about. I'm not excited about failure, but I have to admit that "going out of business" sales present major savings opportunities for the serious shopper. Some stores take their time to really reduce the items to rock-bottom prices; nonetheless, 25 percent off beats paying full price any day. You really need the time and patience to wait for the best deals.

Recently, I found a "going out of business" shoe sale for my children that was better than I could have imagined. Most of the shoes were valued at more than $40, but I paid less than $10 for them. Besides, they were designer shoes, to paint a picture of just how good of a deal I realized. I just wanted good shoes for a good deal, and I most certainly accomplished my objective. I bought 13 pairs of shoes for one son, five for another, and several extras that I gave away to friends. I spent $178.02 for the shoes and saved $426.30 per my

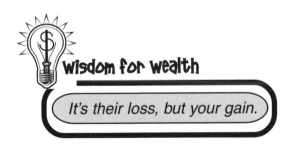

wisdom for wealth

It's their loss, but your gain.

receipt that I'm looking at right now. What a savings! That was one of the best purchases I have made in a long time. My children needed shoes and I was able to buy them for the present and the future.

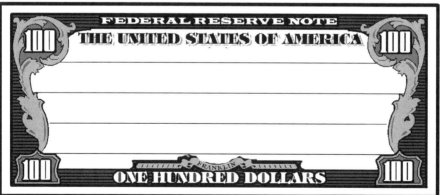

Your *Action Point*

67

---

christmas all year 'round

During the holiday season many retailers amass profits that often cover their entire yearly budget. Even if they fall short of the mark, they certainly aim for it. Think about it: they operate based on a strategic, well-thought-out plan. Their plan is simple--to get as much money from you as possible.

Retailers strategically save some of the latest toys for a holiday debut. Why? Because our kids are going to want the latest and the greatest toys to show off among their peers. There's a lot of pressure to spend during the holiday season. I have to admit that there is something about the Christmas holiday season that puts me in the giving mood perhaps more than any other time of the year.

Who said that you have to purchase Christmas gifts beginning the day after Thanksgiving? You can actually purchase nice gifts year 'round, if you have the discipline to keep them a secret. It may seem like the gift is old to you because you have had it for months, but it will be new to the recipient.

Holiday shopping year 'round gives you time to plan your purchases. It allows you to not feel the crunch of *having* to buy all your gifts within a short period of time. The reality is that most of us end up spending more than we planned. Some people even shop after Christmas because the overstocked sales items are plentiful and cheaper. Most stores sell their excess Christmas inventory at a significantly reduced rate.

If you are thinking about purchasing Christmas gifts year 'round, then whenever an item goes on sale throughout the year you can purchase it at a reduced price. Preserve your budget by spreading out your shopping throughout the year and save, save, save!

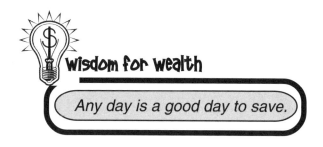

wisdom for wealth

Any day is a good day to save.

Your Action Point

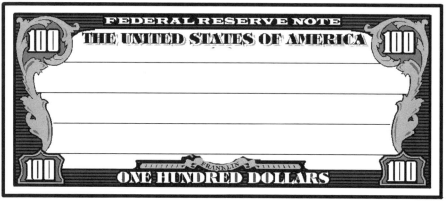

68

price adjustments on sale items

*J*t is customary for most retail stores to give you a price adjustment on items purchased that have been further reduced within ten days or so after your purchase. Years ago a friend of mine informed me about this whole concept of price adjustments. Honestly, the first time that I tried this I was hesitant because it just seemed too good to be true: I make a purchase, and then a few days later, when the item goes on sale, I just take my receipt in and they will refund the difference to me--yeah, right!

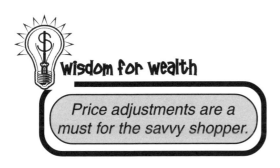

wisdom for wealth

Price adjustments are a must for the savvy shopper.

To my surprise, when I took my receipt into the store I was shocked at how willing the sales-person was to give me my additional savings. I thought she was going to look at me as if I was speaking a foreign lan-guage, but she treated it like it was a very common transaction. I've been a fan of price adjustments ever since.

This is a very good way for savvy shoppers to save. If you are going to shop anyway, then maximize your savings. It is one thing to enjoy a good sale and the spoils that you bring home as a result. It's a double blessing to be able to return to the store, see further reductions on the item, and whip out your receipt to realize additional savings. Receipts are invaluable for this reason.

Price adjustments are a tip that everyone needs to know. Make sure that you pass it along to your friends.

Your *Action Point*

69

a shopper's secret weapon--coupons!

There is nothing like standing behind someone in a check-out line who whips out an additional 15 percent off coupon and wondering, "Where did she get that?" She is using what I call "the shopper's secret weapon"--coupons. This is a true example of "a penny saved is a penny earned." You get the same product at a lower price than everyone else simply because you took the time to redeem the coupon. Consequently, before I even read Sunday's newspaper, I religiously search through it for coupons. My husband informed me that some stores also have printable coupons on the Internet.

One caution in using coupons is that you have to be aware of the expiration date. You may want to get a coupon holder to help you organize your coupons chronologically. Don't forget to check your local phone directory for coupons. There is usually a section designated for coupons from many different stores.

Another source of coupons that I discovered is outlet malls. They usually have magazines containing ads from their various stores with percentage-off coupons. If you don't do your own research you will usually miss out because normally the cashiers aren't going to let you know about the additional savings. It doesn't affect their jobs one way or the other.

I was recently making a purchase at an outlet mall and realized that I didn't have the current outlet magazine. I asked the clerk if their store had an ad in the magazine and she said, "Yes, we have an additional ten percent off coupon in it." I took the time to go to their information center to obtain the magazine. The savings of more than forty dollars was definitely worth the inconvenience.

wisdom for wealth

Coupons: don't leave home without them.

Coupon shopping is part of the "saver's mentality." I once heard a wealthy athlete say that he shops with coupons. In addition, there are people that I know who manage their money well who shop with coupons. Remember, a primary habit of the wealthy is money management. If you don't have to spend the total amount for an item that you are going to purchase anyhow, then why not save by using coupons?

Your Action Point

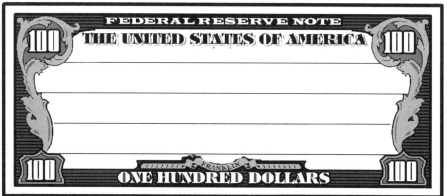

70

avoid the "payment trap"

I used to look at purchases from the perspective of whether I could *afford* the payment. Consider this: just because you can swing the payment doesn't mean that you need to make the purchase. I want you to learn from our mistakes. This tip could save you thousands of dollars.

Eleven years ago we owned a used Mercedes and paid about $5,000 more per year in car payments than necessary because we had the mentality of "I can afford the payments." In retrospect, we couldn't afford the pay-

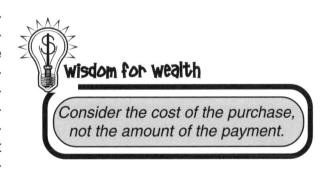

wisdom for wealth

Consider the cost of the purchase, not the amount of the payment.

ments. We would have been much better off purchasing a vehicle with a $400 a month payment, plus cashed in on the savings in car insurance as well. In this scenario, we could have met our transportation needs and had $15,000 in our pockets (in the three years that we owned it). As it turns out, all we had was a car that we really couldn't afford. We made it work, by successfully making the payments each month, but it set us back on our wealth goals. Was it worth it? Only for the wisdom gained, which is now priceless!

It would have been much better to get into something that had a much lower payment and save the difference. If we would have invested that $5,000 a year that we were losing, it could have doubled by now. You know "hindsight is 20/20." As I look back, I would rather have invested that $15,000 and doubled it in eleven years than to have had the experience of driving the Mercedes.

If we could just evaluate potential purchases, without the pull of desires, and just look at each item for what it is we would probably find that we would rather have the money. This is the point of this entire book. Evaluate them now, save your money, and when you look back you'll find a nest egg with your name on it rather than the consequences of an expensive thrill.

Remember, don't look at whether you can afford the payment, but look at the item itself. There is a difference. You cannot afford the item when you sacrifice your savings to pay for it.

71

listen to your inner voice

*T*here are many voices in this world; you need to know which one to follow. Follow your inner voice. Your inner voice is the one that you can faintly hear when you're looking at that drop-dead gorgeous outfit that will fit perfectly. It's the one wheezing, "Don't do it."

There is an old saying that says, "The squeaky wheel gets the oil." It means that the one who makes the most noise usually gets his or her way. I can tell you from experience that your desires are going to have the most profound voice. The voice of immediate gratification will always give you a reason in the moment. Stop and listen! Your inner voice may be saying, "This is not the best purchase for you right now."

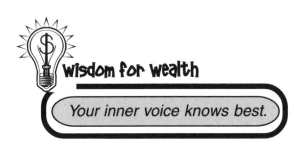

wisdom for wealth

Your inner voice knows best.

Your Action Point

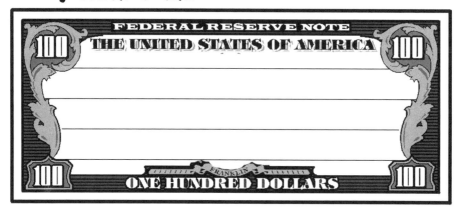

72

mommy, may i have that, pleeeeaaassseee?

I know for sure that I spend more and sometimes much more when I shop with my children. I recognize that for some people avoiding this could be next to impossible, but just be aware of the impact children have on your spending. Awareness is a good thing. I'm always on the receiving end of the begging strategy, "Please, Mom, may I have it, please?" Even if it's a snack, it still costs more than I intended on spending. Think about it: if your children are with you every time that you shop, even at the mall, then you will probably be influenced by them to spend more.

Most children don't understand finances. They just see mom and dad as infinite resources for the many things that they want. Be alert while shopping with your children because they have the potential to pull you in a direction for which you were not financially prepared. Instead, use your shopping outings as a time for training them about finances. My kids always plead for extras every single time I shop with them.

I only have one daughter, and she absolutely loves to shop. She doesn't care if she spends every dime that she has or that I have. Of course, I wouldn't allow this, but if she could, she would. We have gone to the store to spend her birthday money and I would

inform her that if she purchased a particular item that
she wouldn't have any money
left. She simply responded in
a polite way, "So, that's okay."
She loves fashion and she is
a cutie, so I like for her to be
nicely dressed. I also have to
limit what I purchase for her.

wisdom for wealth

*Don't let the kids
get you off track
financially.*

Since I see that she really is
what I call a "feemale," I have begun her money training early.
She is only eleven years old, but she is following my financial
system. When she earns money, she has to set a percentage
aside for savings--period! I'm trying to teach her the balance of
getting some things that you want, along with managing finances
for wealth building.

Your*A*ction *P*oint

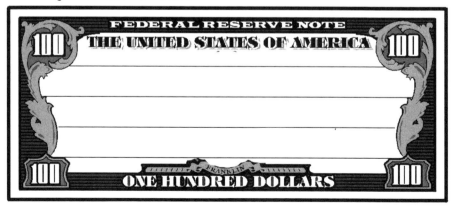

73

beware of wastefulness

*e*xamine your patterns. If you buy clothing and you notice that it sits in the closet for an extended period of time without being worn then change the way that you buy clothes. If you buy food and you notice that it consistently goes to waste, then you must change your philosophy at the point of purchase because it's a wasteful mindset. This is the root of the problem--you didn't think that you were being wasteful at the point of purchase, but there were obviously some things that you didn't consider because it ended up in waste. As you add practicality to whatever else you consider when you purchase, you eliminate the waste.

Wastefulness is deceptive. Are you a waster of goods, money, time or labor? I can look in my closet and see waste, "useless expense." Get this--I am in no way a lavish spender. I buy what I think I need. After it sits in the closet for years unworn, with the tags still attached, then it can be labeled a "useless expense" and; therefore, a waste. For that reason, I recently gave away three sets of clothes (about one hundred items) to individuals who could get some use out of them. Believe it or not, I don't even miss the clothes.

There was a time, I'm almost ashamed to admit it, when I would buy too many groceries only to throw them out at the end of the week. My husband is a vegetarian, which means that I have to buy fresh fruits and vegetables. I thought that I could eliminate those seemingly daily trips to the store, so I would buy everything for the week in one visit. Fresh food must be used quickly or it rots. At that time, I didn't know the value of menu planning so every week I would end up in the same position. I bought what I thought I'd cook only to watch it sit in the fridge and grow hair. This was a wasteful habit.

wisdom for wealth

Eliminate waste and save.

My husband witnessed me throwing away food once and commented, "You need to just shop more often because this isn't good." From then on, I made the necessary adjustments. I am not saying that I'm perfect yet, but I am doing 99.99 percent better.

Examine your ways when it comes to any area of consumption--food, energy, time, or whatever--to see if you can find any area where you can become more frugal. You just might be surprised at what you find. Whatever you find, save!

Your Action Point

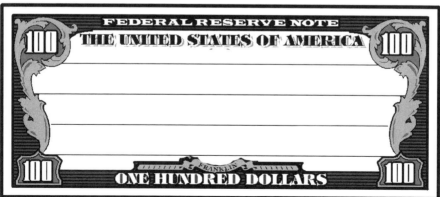

74

"seasons" of saving

*R*etailers determine, based on what is most profitable for them, when to feature season-specific items. So you in turn, can determine (based on what's most profitable for you) when to purchase these season-specific items. You'll find that when retailers bring in items for the next season, they will sell items from the previous season at a greatly reduced price; therefore, February and March may be the best time to buy a snow blower, for example, because retailers are featuring Spring gardening equipment during this time.

wisdom for wealth

Purchase when it's to your best advantage.

I have experienced my greatest savings with this strategy in buying clothes. It seems as though stores are bringing in their line for a particular season earlier and earlier. Doing this, I have purchased the kids' entire summer wardrobe for up to 75 percent savings. I tucked them away in storage bins and was full of joy the following year just going downstairs for their reduced price clothing instead of to the mall to pay full price in the season of need. You could potentially save thousands of dollars a year this way.

Your Action Point

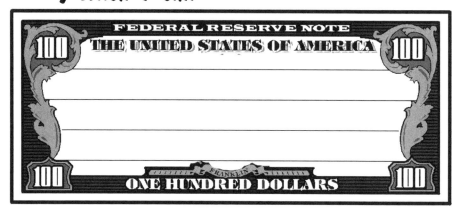

FEDERAL RESERVE NOTE
THE UNITED STATES OF AMERICA
100   100
100   100
ONE HUNDRED DOLLARS

75

---

deal or no deal?

*W*hile walking through the store, you see an unadvertised clearance sale that just blows you away. It is the item that you can use and it is dirt cheap. You throw it in your cart and head for the checkout. What a deal! Or, is it? If it's an untimely purchase, then it is not a deal for you. You could have saved that money.

I had a friend who recently found a good sale on ink for her printer. She purchased the items with joy because she felt as though it was a good deal. When she thought about it, she realized that it really didn't make sense for her to purchase the cartridges, even though they were on sale, because her printer wasn't even working. She was even happier when she returned the items and got her $58 back that she was able to apply toward something else for which she otherwise would not have had the money.

I love to get good deals so much so that I would purchase "good deal" items that I couldn't use and give them away. Some people like to spend--period! I was one of them when it came to good deals. Giving is a virtue, but debt isn't. Every deal is not a deal, especially if it costs you your savings. We are accustomed to rejoicing about how much we saved on "deals;" but you could have saved the entire $150 or whatever the amount was that you spent.

My point is that a "good deal" doesn't mean that you have to "deal." You can let the item go or leave it on the rack.

I understand the "good deal" mentality, but remember, there are two ways to look at a deal. Good deals can cost you or save you. It costs you when you don't really need it, but you buy it simply because it is such a good deal, as my friend did. It saves you when you recognize that it is a good deal, but you are able to walk away and keep your money in your pocket.

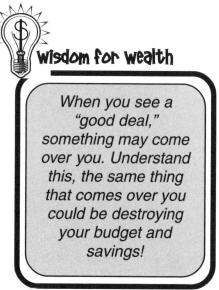

wisdom for wealth

When you see a "good deal," something may come over you. Understand this, the same thing that comes over you could be destroying your budget and savings!

You must address this "good deal" mentality if you are going to be a saver. It leaves you vulnerable to the sales tactic of making something seem like a good deal to inspire you to make the purchase. Oftentimes a store or vendor will start out at an inflated price on an item and take you through the process of reducing it right there, just to make you feel like you are getting a good deal.

Your Action Point

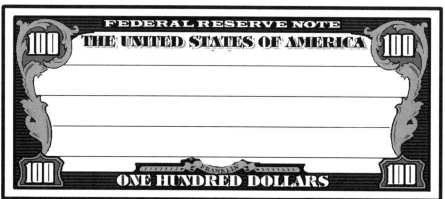

76

i thirst

*B*uying bottled drinking water can cost more than you think, depending on how and where you buy it. Water is one item that seems as though it should be free. You might save on water in the long run by buying a water system or purifier rather than buying bottled water.

If you decide that buying water is a must for you, then here are some ways to save. I buy water because my home has well water. I buy bottled water when it's on sale. That's one way to save. The best way that I've found to save is to buy water by the gallon.

You can also realize significant savings if you buy the store brand versus name brand water. The store brand gallon that I buy is $0.69, but the name brand gallon is $1.09. I priced a name brand 24-pack of water at $4.50 on sale. It amounted to a little over three gallons. Three

wisdom for wealth

Change quantities for quality savings.

gallons at $0.69 equals $2.07. I realized a minimum of $2.43 savings. Ounce for ounce, it costs less to buy water by the gallon. If you drink a gallon of water per day, this will save you nearly $300 a year.

If you are paying one dollar or more at a convenience store per 16 ounce bottle of water, then you need to recognize that it is the convenience that is costing you. You'll save money by purchasing water containers and refilling them, as I did, with your $0.69 per gallon water. This affords you savings over and over and over again.

Your*A*ction *P*oint

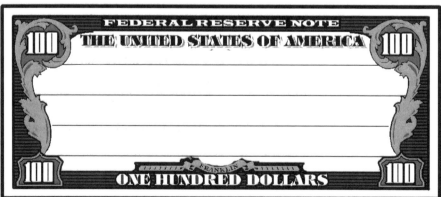

77

what's love got to do with it?

One of my greatest virtues is loyalty. I believe in finding something of good quality and sticking with it. I'm in it for the long haul. That's a wonderful virtue in relationships, but not so wonderful for saving. At some point I asked myself, "Why do you buy certain brands?" I discovered that most of the brand loyalty was simply based on products that my mother used. The products were quality, but so are others.

Is there a significant enough difference in the quality to justify you habitually paying more? You want to maintain a certain level of quality, so identify a pool of brands that will accomplish that goal. Then, watch for coupons and sales to minimize your expense for that product. Laundry detergent is a good example of this; there is usually some high quality laundry detergent on sale. I grew up using a certain brand, but since I've em-

wisdom for wealth

Be loyal to your financial goals. If the brand is loyal to you in savings, then buy it; if it costs you more, then leave it!

ployed the strategies listed above, I haven't noticed the difference in the performance of these products, but I have noticed a difference in the savings. Brand loyalty can cause you to habitually pay more and to miss out on significant cyclical savings that comparable products offer. When my brand is on sale, for less than the comparable brands, then I put it in the shopping cart. If it is not, then a less popular brand looks good to me.

I now place my loyalty where it belongs, with my family's financial future. Companies don't have loyalty toward you. They just want to make a sale. The only good deal is a deal that's good for everybody. I'm not so attached to a particular brand name that I can't pass it by to save.

Your*A*ction *P*oint

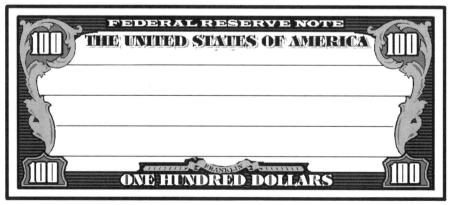

78

avoid the "major purchase" pit

People rarely sell used items that are in perfect condition. If it's for sale, then there is usually some hidden flaw or it's no longer useful. It could be masked by aesthetics. It is advantageous to investigate common problems with used items.

wisdom for wealth

Inspect before you write the check.

I know people who have financed used cars with more than 125,000 miles on them. That is asking for trouble. The previous owner likely sold the car in the first place to avoid the impending major maintenance problems. It was on its way to becoming a money trap. Once you fix one thing, then another thing falls apart. It is common for those cars to spend more time in the repair shop than on the road. Some owners can't afford to get the car fixed and make the payments. They are just stuck. The car may look perfect, but there's a major problem looming right around the corner.

When purchasing a previously owned home, it is always advisable to get an inspection on the infrastructure of the house. Check the roof and basement for leaks, and check the plumbing, electric, heating and cooling systems for flaws and for termites. If you purchase a house that needs work in any one of these areas, you will be out of thousands of dollars and the house may be uninhabitable. As a rule, if you are buying a used big ticket item, then have an expert check it out to make sure that you are not buying somebody else's problem.

Your*A*ction *P*oint

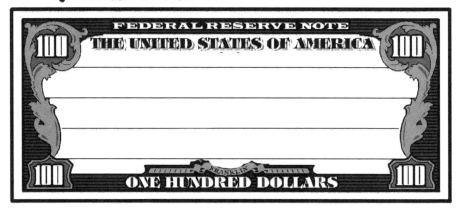

79

---

reject
rent-to-own!

*I*n my opinion, deciding to rent-to-own is one of the worst financial decisions that one could make, other than credit card debt. Renting to own puts you further into the financial "black hole." I priced a washer at a "Rent-to-Own" store. The weekly payments were very affordable, $13.99 per week. After paying those payments for 91 weeks, you would own the washer, but at triple the standard department store price!

The "Rent-to-Own" store also offered "90 days same as cash." The price for the washer was still nearly $250 more than the price of the same item in the other store that I researched. If you can get the item in 90 days, then put the money aside and purchase it from a store that specializes in the item. It may require a little patience to wait, but the savings will be worth the wait.

$$\$13.99 \times 91 = \$1,273.09$$
90 days, same as cash was $636.55
department store cost was $399.99

"Rent-to-Own" is for people who probably consistently make bad financial decisions or those who just cannot see their options. "Rent-to-Own" items seem to solve a problem in the short-run. It is like financially "going out of the world backwards," as this ex-

pression is used. If you cannot afford to make the purchase in the first place, you
surely cannot afford to pay for
it three times over.

wisdom for wealth

*Delay and avoid
financial disasters.*

Reject the concept of "Rent-to-
Own." The reason they can
give you the item for "ninety
days same as cash" is be-
cause they have already added the profit to the price. The "Rent-
to-Own" seller is willing to wait for the profit; you must be willing to
wait for your benefit.

Your *Action Point*

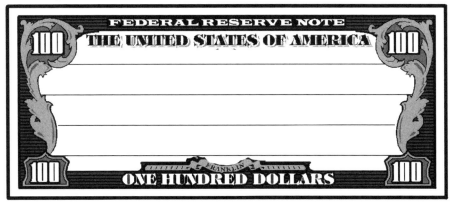

80

Compare prices before buying

*O*ur parents probably taught us not to compare one person to another, but that principle doesn't apply to things. It's wise to compare. Why pay more for the exact same item which you can purchase for less? One of the best comparison tools is the local newspaper. The ads allow you to compare while in the comfort of your home. You can make a few calls to retailers beforehand. This affords you time to think about the best approach for the purchase. The Internet is also a great tool for comparing prices.

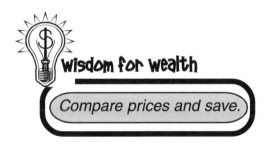

wisdom for wealth

Compare prices and save.

Sometimes I may find a better deal in a store that I normally don't patronize. Don't allow yourself to become loyal to a store if it doesn't offer the best savings. Declare your loyalty to your wallet! It's easy to become comfortable shopping in a particular place just out of habit. Wake up! Be alert! Pay attention to what you are spending in the marketplace. Because of this, I purchase the item from that store if it makes more sense financially.

The bottom-line is your bottom-line. The most important part of comparison shopping is realizing the savings. Take the difference that you saved by doing a little research and deposit it into your savings account.

Your*A*ction *P*oint

81

resale

*C*heck the resale shops in your area for possible savings. There are adult and children's shops that may work for you. I've even been in resale shops that offer high-end designer outfits for a reasonable price.

wisdom for wealth

Don't let pride keep you from the resale store; resale stores can save you money.

You can also sell your used clothing to these shops because once you've worn them, technically, they don't have any real value except what a person will pay for them. Now that there are shops that specialize in used clothing, you may be able to get something back, rather than letting the clothes sit in your closet with no monetary value.

When I first got married, to my surprise, my husband shopped at resale stores. He had his special shops that he would frequent. That was new to me. I was not a shopper for used clothing. It worked for him and our budget at the time so I didn't influence him otherwise.

You can also resell by hosting your own garage sale. Price your items to get rid of them; go for quantity, not the big kill.

Your*A*ction *P*oint

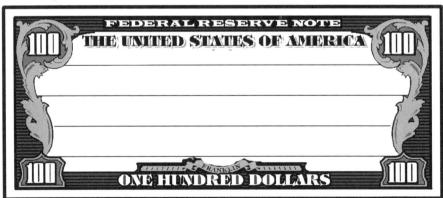

82

---

the thrifty shopper

*T*hrift stores can also be great for purchasing items for less. There is a bread thrift store down the street from me that I visit. This is a way to save because bread is expensive in my opinion. There is no shame in my game.

To my surprise, thrift stores carry brand name items for less. This is a good way to save on items that you would normally purchase for full price at a grocery store.

Find the nearest thrift stores in your area and give them a visit to see if they carry items that you use for less. The fact that it's a thrift store doesn't mean that the items are lesser quality. You might be pleasantly surprised by what you find.

wisdom for wealth

Shop at the thrift store and save.

Your Action Point

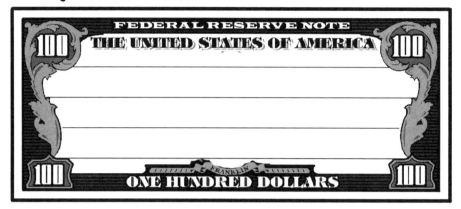

83

garage/estate sales

*O*ur subdivision has garage sales every summer. Those sales draw major traffic into the community. Garage sale attendees are bargain shoppers in a league of their own. You never know what you might find at a garage or an estate sale. They are great for browsing. I recently purchased a ping pong table for $100 at an estate sale. It was in excellent condition. My husband looked on the Internet and found that the same table, purchased new, would cost around $800. I realized a savings of $700--87.5 percent!

Last year I had in mind some furniture that I desired to purchase. I shopped and compared prices, but found the furniture stores too expensive. So I decided to wait. At an estate sale I found that furniture and in all saved more than $2,400. Everything looks new. I'd say that it was worth the wait.

I was also looking for a bookcase for a particular area of my home to help

wisdom for wealth

You can find quality items at great prices at garage and estate sales.

with organization. I priced one at a local retailer and it would have cost about $250. I decided to wait. At the same estate sale I found a bookcase, in mint condition, for $60.

That's the way to shop. Just make sure that you don't overspend at this type of sale as well. It can be tempting to buy everything even if you don't really have a use for it. Also, don't buy anyone's "junk:" examine quality to ensure longevity of use.

Your*A*ction *P*oint

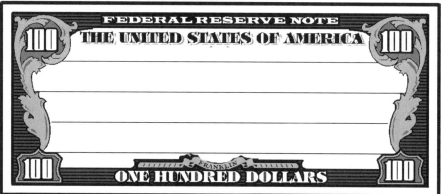

84

do i need this?

Answering the question, "Do I need this?" is the very key to unlocking your savings ability. When I look back at financial decisions that have cost me dearly, I wish that I would have asked myself that question. I don't think that my results would have been the same. I now know better.

Purchasing large ticket items at the wrong time or for the wrong reason can throw your finances off for years. What's really at stake is your savings. The purchase seems affordable, but it can drain your finances.

wisdom for wealth

Don't hobble your savings plan unnecessarily.

Affordability is a tricky thing. It has little to do with your ability to make the monthly payment and everything to do with watching the money that you would have saved, disappear. If instead of buying a new luxury vehicle for $800 a month, you buy a slightly used midsize vehicle at $250 a month and save the difference of $550, you would realize a significant boost in your savings program. Don't hobble your savings plan. You'll be amazed at what

you can actually live without. One decision can make you or break
you when it comes to savings.

Your*A*ction *P*oint

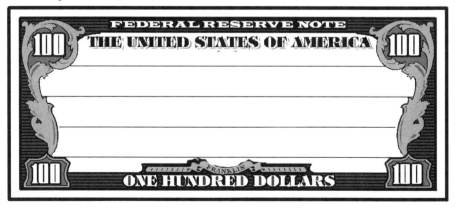

85

use discounts

*R*emember, whatever you don't spend you can save. Discounts offer a variety of savings. Insurance companies, like AAA, offer savings to its members on hotels, restaurants, car rentals, and also on retail store purchases. When making hotel reservations ask for the discounted rates. It will usually amount to a significant savings of at least 10 percent. This is a roadside membership which may be purchased for less than $50 per year. You don't have to have their auto insurance to join. Your savings will more than cover your membership fee.

wisdom for wealth

A discount used is money saved.

A major benefit is that roadside service is national and offers other free services. This includes things like towing and jump starts for when your car breaks down or just won't start.

For those who are over the age of 55, you can join AARP (American Association of Retired Persons) which also offers significant discounts for goods and services.

There are many discounts available; a little research can amount to significant savings. Here's an example: I purchased some mattresses from a local store and after the fact learned that the store offered a 10 percent discount for AAA members. I quickly took my receipt back and received a $42 check in return. What a deal!

Your**A**ction **P**oint

86

utilize friendships

When it comes to items like clothing I don't consider myself a "real shopper." I have been around women who are "real shoppers," and they are absolutely amazing to watch. It is almost like something comes over them to help them shop. These women are usually aware of the best time and right place to find the best deals for most of my clothing needs. These "real shoppers" know the "mark-down-cycles," when items are going to be further reduced and by how much.

wisdom for wealth

*A friend,
when you're in need,
is a friend indeed.*

For this reason I recommend that you do as I do: call upon friends who are "real shoppers," and let them direct you to the best deals.

This also applies to people who are very knowledgeable in areas such as computers, appliances, and vehicles. They may be able to point you to the greatest savings.

Since I don't frequent the malls as much as certain friends, when I need to shop, I rely on those who know exactly where to find the real deals. This saves time and money. When I need school uniforms or supplies for the kids, I call a particular friend. When I need shoes, I call another friend. When I need a computer or related items, I call yet another friend. They never fail to inform me of the best places to save.

Check out your friends. Many people have a shopping specialty and valuable knowledge about savings. Sometimes we shop with our limited knowledge and miss out on great deals. Making a few phone calls to friends could point you in the right direction and cause you to realize tremendous savings.

Your*A*ction *P*oint

87

the "dollar store" syndrome

*L*et me start by saying, it's not just a dollar! It's usually several dollars that you spend at the dollar store. Don't be fooled by the concept. I've known people to spend $50 at the dollar store with an "it's just a dollar" mentality.

Coincidently, I just spoke with a friend who told me that she stopped to calculate her spending habits over a month's time. She kept all of her receipts from her purchases. To her surprise, she was spending an average of $40 per week at the dollar store. The reason she was frequenting the dollar store so often is that she had the mentality that it was only a dollar. Of course, it was an eye-opener to her and she amended her ways as a result.

Quality is often an issue when shopping for dollar items. I once bought some dishwashing liquid at a dollar store. It seemed like water. It lacked the potency of the dish soaps that I was accustomed to using. With the aid of a coupon, I could have purchased my normal dish soap for a dollar.

I do understand that there are some quality brand name items that you can also find at a dollar store. The key is to buy what you went in to purchase, and if you don't need it or haven't budgeted for it, then leave it. Don't get caught in the "dollar trap."

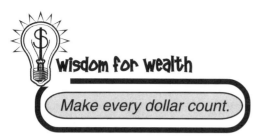

wisdom for wealth

Make every dollar count.

If the dollar store is the place for you to find good, quality items for less, then go for it. Just don't use the dollar store as a place to overspend. Dollars go quickly in the dollar store.

Your*A*ction *P*oint

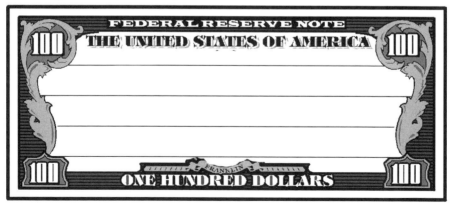

88

---

a "spending fast"

*T*here's no quicker way to save than not to spend. You may wonder, "What is the use in working hard if you can't enjoy the fruit of your labor?" You're right. You won't get an argument from me. I absolutely think that you should enjoy the fruit of your labor. I'm just saying don't eat all of the fruit. Have some leftovers. Laying aside savings provides financial defense that shields you against the "rainy day" and "lean seasons," both of which are coming. A savings nest gives you options and allows you to establish long-term financial strength or wealth.

One strategy is to go on what I call a "spending fast." A spending fast is where for a set period of time, you abstain from purchasing nonessential items. This is where you fast things like the malls, your favorite snacks, costly entertainment, and dining out with a goal of maximizing your savings.

The main purpose of a "spending fast" is to help you become more in tune with your spending habits. It is said that anything that you do consistently for 21 days becomes a habit. By taking a spending break, it allows you to establish new habits: good financial management skills, savings ability, and discipline. I have a friend who challenged herself to see how long she could go without spending any money. She was pleased to find that she went three days without spending a dime. She purchased her essentials for the week and tested herself to see if she could exercise the disci-pline not to spend on anything extra. She was ecstatic to find out that she really didn't have to spend money every day.

wisdom for wealth

Fast and watch your money grow.

Often, the people who don't feel as if they have enough money to save do not realize the money they are spending on nonessential items can be saved. There was probably a time in your life when you really didn't have money to spend, mine was while I was in college--five dollars was a lot of money. Not spending was habitual because you didn't have a choice. Pretend that you don't really have money to spend and see how much you can save.

You may want to try this strategy for a couple of weeks or a month and see what results it produces. If you really like your results, fast longer and watch your money grow faster.

Your Action Point

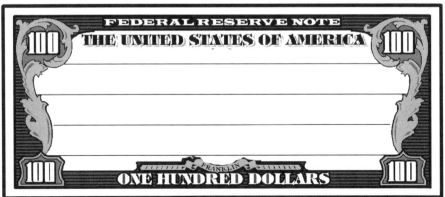

89

do not
procrastinate

*P*rocrastination is costly. It's like pushing things forward into your future because you do not want to deal with them today. The reality is that we live in a world governed by time. If you habitually procrastinate then you may miss out on a lot of savings.

Procrastination is the "I'm going to" (future) or "I should have" (past) mentality. It's a habit that you can't afford. By the time you motivate yourself, the deals may be long gone.

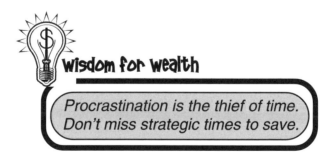

wisdom for wealth

Procrastination is the thief of time.
Don't miss strategic times to save.

I saw an ad for some beautiful reasonably priced china. I needed to upgrade my china due to the amount of entertaining that my lifestyle requires. By the time I arrived at the store all of the china was gone. The astute shoppers had left with their bags full, and I departed empty-handed.

It takes too long for procrastinators to make the decision to act. I'm referring to purchases that you really need. Remember, the longer you take, the more you may lose. Procrastination can have a serious impact on savings in multiple areas. Saving is often about taking advantage of opportunities. Opportunities come in a window and once the window is closed the opportunity is gone.

A friend told me how she could have saved thousands of dollars with her company's savings plan, but procrastination cost her dearly. Her coworker urged her to move on it, but it took her years to follow his advice. That is something that she sorely regrets to this day.

Your*A*ction *P*oint

90

beware of emotional spending

*e*motions change rapidly. It is their nature. The reason that you must be watchful of emotional spending is that emotions usually aren't tied to sensible logic. Not thinking can cost you a bundle.

When you emotionally spend you're lax because you're "under the influence." Something has stimulated your emotions, and your illogical emotions have provoked your spending.

If you just want to celebrate, then think of ways to do it that don't cost money. If you're angry, then exercise rigorously. If you're sad, then listen to a good motivational tape. The bottom-line is, do not respond to your emotions by spending.

wisdom for wealth

Guard your pocketbook from your emotions.

Pleasure purchases cannot compensate for life's disappointments. All they do is add insult to injury by weakening you financially. Don't do something that you'll later regret. Emotional spending can throw your financial future into a tailspin.

Ask yourself a series of questions like "Can I wait? Do I really need it? Why am I really purchasing this?" By the time you have answered them, you may get a hold of yourself.

Your*A*ction *P*oint

91

ignore sales calls

We are bombarded by salespeople. We receive calls that we did not request and that we do not want to entertain. Sometimes we are even faced with an occasional knock on the door that catches us off-guard. Sales pitches are all around us.

Who says that you have to answer? My husband would answer the phone call of a salesperson and immediately respond, "I'm not interested." The person would literally be dumbfounded. The response would be, "How do you know? You haven't even heard what I have to say." My husband would graciously say, "If I wanted what you're offering, I would have called you." We may not have the guts to handle those kind of salespeople like that. If not, then just ignore their call.

I have had salespeople call me and when I told them that I wasn't interested they would hang up in my face. How rude to call my house and just hang up in my face because I am not interested in the product. That kind of behavior turns me off. I should have the right to decline the offer and still be respected. There are other salespeople whom you tell *no* and they keep talking as if you never said *no*. Then you say "No thank you" and they still persist. In that case, my husband says goodbye and hangs up, because the person doesn't hear "No."

I look at the caller ID and if it registers as "unknown," "blocked," or "out of area," that's my clue that I want to ignore those calls. A caller ID is good for tracking unwanted sales calls. When the "no call" list came out to protect consumers from telemarketers we immediately enrolled. For those who have not registered yet the web address is www.telemarketing.donotcall.gov. The Federal Trade Commission does allow cell phone users to add their numbers to the National Do Not Call Registry--the same one already in force for landlines--either via the Web or by calling 1-888-382-1222. My husband and I came to an agreement some time ago that neither of us would ever make a decision--without the other--about making a purchase based on a "phone pitch." This helped safe guard us from the pressure pitch and purchasing untimely or unneeded items.

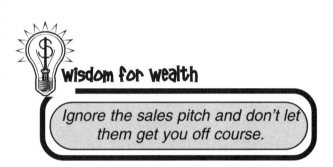

wisdom for wealth

Ignore the sales pitch and don't let them get you off course.

Your *Action Point*

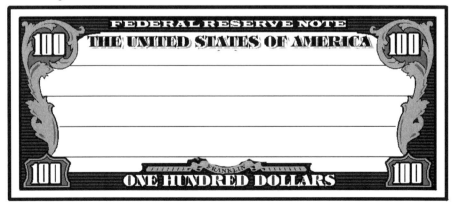

92

don't take the bait--negotiate

*e*very transaction contains two desires: the seller's desire to sell for a profit and the consumer's desire to own. Whoever controls his or her desire the best gets the most out of the transaction. Refrain from buying anything from the first place that you shop. There's usually someone who wants to sell it more which is indicated by his or her cheaper price. When you control your desire to buy you'll find somebody who's more desperate to sell.

Transactions usually have room for negotiation. You can easily check by asking, "Is this your best price?" Inquire about specials. Often, salespeople don't tell you about specials, but they will allow you to pay full price for the item. They're not being malicious. They're just doing their jobs.

wisdom for wealth

Maintain the power when you purchase.

The key to negotiation is desire. The ability to control your desire is the ability to get the most out of your purchase. If the seller will not give you the lowest price then maybe he or she will throw something else in. If you buy a suit, see if they will throw in a shirt or a belt free. If you buy multiple units, ask the seller to cut you a deal.

My philosophy is, "I want it, but at my price;" therefore, I'm willing to wait for it, even if it takes years. For years we were planning to make a major purchase. The people with whom we were working weren't really willing to negotiate on the price. After assessing the cost of what we would have to pay, we determined that it was more than we were willing to commit to paying. My husband and I decided that we weren't desperate for the item and were willing to wait to make the purchase. We ended up purchasing the item for one fourth the price that we would have had we not exercised patience. Control your desires and save, save, save.

Your *A*ction *P*oint

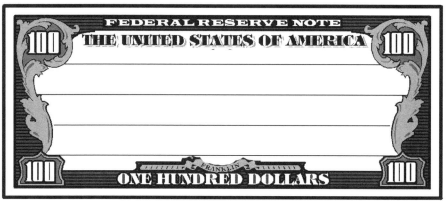

93

---

to co-sign or
not to co-sign?

Avoid co-signing at all costs. If someone needs a co-signer, could it be that he or she cannot afford the item? If the lender recognizes this instability, why don't you?

Once you sign on the dotted line, the creditor holds you equally responsible for the debt. If the debt is unpaid or not paid in a timely manner by the original borrower, then it is reflected on your credit report.

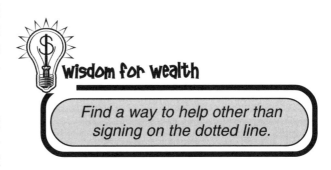

wisdom for wealth

Find a way to help other than signing on the dotted line.

By the time that you, as the co-signer, find out there's a problem, it's usually too late. You will have to assume the debt. If you don't fulfill the obligation, you suffer as if you were the originator of the debt. Co-signing puts you in a very vulnerable position. You have virtually no control, but all of the responsibility.

This is one principle I have enforced in my life. I try to think of other options or ways to help without signing on the dotted line. You may have a wonderful relationship with the person who may ask you for this favor, but you never know how people handle their business. Let their business remain their business. Don't get entangled in a net from which there is no escape.

Your*A*ction *P*oint

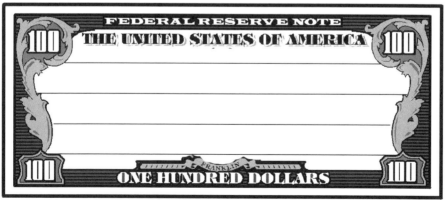

94

"may i have that?"

Pay attention to things that people don't use. Sometimes they have things lying around that they just don't know what to do with. Help them out! Ask for it. You're solving their problem and yours. Their problem is what to do with it and yours is how to keep your money. They may be surprised that you asked, maybe even shocked, but most of the time it's only because they never considered giving it away.

I know someone who helped a business pack its inventory and close. He noticed brand new garbage cans and a pallet of unopened reams of office paper sitting in the corner. He asked, "What are you going to do with that?" The person in charge said, "I don't know." He asked, "May I have that?" She said, "Sure, that's a great idea; just take it." Those items would have easily cost him $200.

Asking for things that are not considered the usual "free stuff" takes grace. Never demand because you don't deserve anything, even if you have spent a lot of money over the years with that business. Be gracious when you ask and be gracious when you hear the answer. Grace stretches a lot farther than money.

Being in the right place at the right time is priceless, and asking the question, "May I have that?" in the right place and time is golden. Do not be afraid to ask for anything. Besides, what are you afraid of—No? They're not rejecting you. They're rejecting the request.

Just by asking you can get what you want, eventually; a house, land, tools, appliances, etc. The sky is the limit. Keep asking the question and get use to hearing, "No." It makes it even more exhilarating when you hear, "Yes."

wisdom for wealth

Don't despise free items.

Your *Action Point*

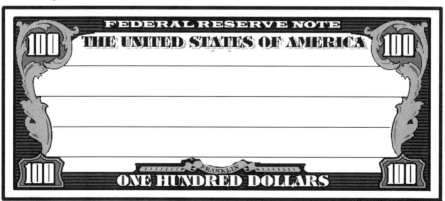

95

subscriptions

Subscriptions save you money as opposed to buying the magazine off of the rack. I just paid $4.50 for a monthly magazine that caught my interest. I found out that a year's subscription to the magazine only costs around fifteen dollars.

On the other hand, if you are subscribing to magazines and newspapers or other publications and you're not really using them, then cut the subscription and save all together.

You may have a service-oriented business that uses magazines as "good reading" to occupy clients who wait. This is a good use of the savings that subscriptions afford. I read of one guy who collected subscriptions of a particular magazine for historic reasons.

wisdom for wealth

Cancel subscriptions, such as newspapers or magazines, which you are not using.

Whatever you choose, just make sure you're getting your money's worth. Often a vendor offers you a "free" subscription for a period of time, but you have to call and cancel or after the period of time you will be charged for it. This is a common ploy used by salespeople who are aware of our busy lives. Salespeople are betting on the fact that most of us are not going to remember that three months from now we need to call and cancel a subscription. So to be safe say, "No" up front and save.

Your Action Point

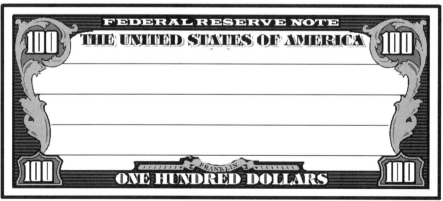

Part V

Investments

96

research the best savings programs

My husband and I would deposit money in the bank without asking many questions. We blindly put our trust in the interest that the bank offered. One day, it finally dawned on us that we should be letting our money work for us, rather than just letting it sit in a bank gaining little or no interest.

It is important to keep some money "liquid" or available in case of an emergency, but seek high interest-bearing accounts. Let your money accumulate interest as it sits. There are multiple savings vehicles that can help fulfill your savings goals: such as CDs, IRA's, mutual funds, money market accounts, and insurance investment vehicles.

One thing to consider is the level of risk. How much risk are you in a position to endure? The rule of thumb is the higher the risk, the higher the return, the lower the risk, the lower the return. Examine interest rates, the tax structure and fees. Find out the best vehicles that will get you where you want to go.

Remember, the banks invest your money for their profit. If they can make money off of your money then so can you. Research investments and learn how to take control of your financial future.

All investments are not for everybody. Investing is an individual decision consisting of many variables. Also, different financial products are introduced all of the time. Banks have specials and even pay you to open certain savings accounts. They pay interest based on the amount that you deposit. One local bank had a special where it offered 5 percent interest for six months as well as a $50 gift certificate upon opening an account with a certain amount. We took advantage of this deal.

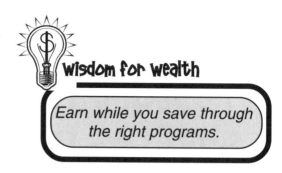

wisdom for wealth

Earn while you save through the right programs.

Your*A*ction *P*oint

97

look before you leap

J'm not afraid to admit it--I'm an opportunist, especially when it comes to shopping and saving. In fact, I rather like it. Some days it seems as if I can spot an opportunity coming from a mile away. If you're an opportunist also, then welcome to the club! Here is where the rubber meets the road for the opportunist, though: you must examine opportunities closely before you commit. In other words, "Look before you leap." Inherent in every opportunity is a balance of gain and costs.

Many times friends and family bring "the" opportunity to you, parading individuals who have made "big money" before you to peak your interest. Most opportunities have fees and product costs. The funny thing about this is that all of the opportunities that I have looked at seemed good. I finally got the picture: just because it's good doesn't mean it's good for me. I have plunged into at least six opportunities over the years and the upside is that I've learned from each one of them. The downside is that I didn't profit from most of them. There was a particular opportunity in which I have realized tremendous gain. It has served as one of my savings vehicles.

All I'm advising is that before you "leap," consider the cost. There may be costs for product, materials, attending meetings, gas,

Internet service, packaging and postage. Take a really good look within and reach a quality decision. If, from past experience, you've invested in opportunities with little yield for your effort then certain kinds of opportunities may not be your niche. Before you get involved in any opportunity, you need to thoroughly review it and come to a good understanding of the compensation plan, which details when and how much you get paid. If, from past experience, you know that your tendency is to join in on a business venture, but not really work it then you can save yourself some money by not joining or starting. If you think that you can leverage your time and make a significant profit, then go for it if it's the right thing at the right time.

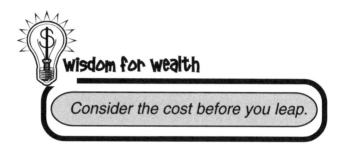

wisdom for wealth

Consider the cost before you leap.

Your*Action Point*

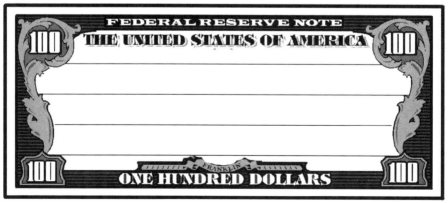

98

---

maximize your company's savings plan

My husband previously worked for a company with a savings plan that matched its employees' contributions up to 5 percent. To his regret, he didn't maximize the plan as he was advised by a wise supervisor. He did not really understand the benefit; therefore, he missed out on a great opportunity to get ahead.

He only put in the minimum amount, 1 percent. He admits that he was young and dumb then. That decision still hurts even today. For an overall investment of $3,000 he gained $16,000 through the program. He still kicks himself about not having invested more as he was advised. Don't follow his mistake! Let me help you. Take time today to research your company's savings plan and maximize it, especially if your company matches your investment dollars. That is an automatic, immediate 100 percent return on your money plus whatever it gains in the market. This will put you years ahead of the game.

To put this in perspective, a 15%-20% return in a year is considered great. My husband withdrew the money after transitioning out of that job and received an average of $1,600 for ten years. Had he invested the maximum, he would have gained at least $80,000 and gotten an $8,000 per year payout. How could he

Get the maximum bang
for your savings buck.

have made so much? Good question. There are three things happening here: you are investing before-tax dollars; your company is matching your dollars, and so automatically you get a 100 percent return on your money; and you are investing it at a guaranteed rate of return. Your money grows exponentially. You only pay taxes on the return when you decide to take the money out at your current tax rate.

The problem is that my husband was so short-sighted in this matter. He wanted his money right away. He did not need it and could have done without it. By the way, he could have given the maximum and not missed it at all.

Your Action Point

99

---

dump the lumps

Whether you receive expected or unexpected large amounts of money at once, "dump the lumps." It's hard to pull lump sums back together when you've spent them. Protect what you're not expecting. Lump sums are an excellent incentive to save.

You can get better interest rates on larger amounts of money and this will increase your savings over time. Large sums grow faster. They can put you on course financially to boost your savings plan. You may want to give yourself a small reward out of your lump sum, but beware that just as fast as it came into your life, it can leave.

You can "dump the lumps" in a short-term savings plan which at least gives you time to think about what the best and wisest move is for you. You can put it in a safe savings vehicle for a year that's earning you 5 percent interest. Your money is growing while you are growing. In other words, you may be more mature and even wiser a year down the road.

Most of the things that we buy depreciate, which means we have spent hard earned money on things that lose value. Very soon after the purchase, we do not have the asset or the financial strength to show for it. "Dump the lumps," whether they are expected or unexpected and you will be glad that you did.

From our experience lump sums usually come outside of the normal flow of income. If you put them in with the rest of your money, they have great potential to get lost in the shuffle.

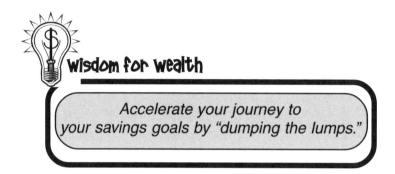

wisdom for wealth

Accelerate your journey to your savings goals by "dumping the lumps."

Your Action Point

100

---

cash value life insurance

J have learned how to strategically use cash value life insurance policies, such as whole life and universal life to build wealth. In the past, many financial service professionals have advised against using life insurance as an investment vehicle; however, several financially astute individuals are taking advantage of the benefits of cash value life insurance policies. Such polices serve the traditional purpose of death benefit while providing liquid cash reserves at a good rate of return.

Keep in mind, this is a *long-term* investment vehicle. Once you acquire enough money in the savings portion (cash value) of the policy, the premium will no longer be required. One uniqueness of such policies is their tax-free withdrawal structure. Withdrawals are considered loans against your death benefit, so they may reduce your death benefit in the short run, but your cash value is maintained and continues to grow while you use the money for whatever purpose that you desire. As you pay the loan back, with interest, the principle and the interest payment goes back to your policy. In essence, you are borrowing from yourself.

I have had term life insurance for years. Term is the least expensive life insurance and it is strictly for protection with no investment value. These policies aren't designed for you to accumulate any cash reserves. The premiums paid aren't set aside in an interest-bearing account for you to receive later. The only pay out for these policies is at the time of death.

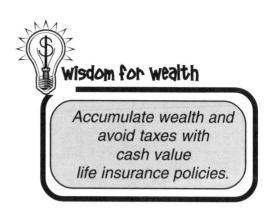

Things to be aware of: there are administrative fees associated with cash value life insurance policies. Interest rates are adjusted annually. As a short-term investment, you will earn very little on such an account. The ability to accumulate large amounts of money and avoid taxes makes this a very attractive long-term savings vehicle.

Your*Action Point*

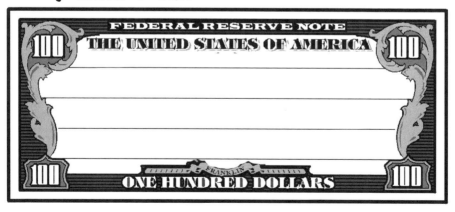

101

---

start today--
just do it!

Some people know everything that they need to know about making their savings grow. They may know it, but they haven't incorporated the necessary habits into their lives.

Have you ever talked to someone who made it clear that he or she already knows what you are about to say? Let me call it the "know-it-all syndrome." It feels as if you are traveling down a one-way street. If the person knows so much, then why isn't

wisdom for wealth

Knowledge doesn't translate to savings; saving does.

there more evidence of his or her knowledge showing up in the person's life? This knowledge should have practical use. It is when you act on what you know that you get results. If you know everything and still aren't saving, my counsel is this: "on your mark, get set, SAVE!"

If you are already using the tips that I have shared in this book, and you have the financial strength that you desire--all that you need and a lot left over--then pass this along to a friend or associate in need. Be blessed on your journey to financial strength through maximized savings!

Your**A**ction **P**oint

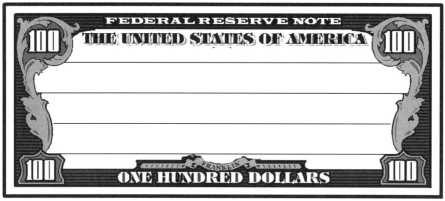

Serious Savers
Starter Kit

take control of your financial future!

VISIT www.101waysyoucansave.com

and RECEIVE;

- **Discounts**
- **Coupons**
- **Savings tip of the month**
- *And* **much, much more**

101 ways you can save money